"Bowling shares his obv ancient churches and canals, presenting an easy-to-use manual peppered with small tidbits of Venetian history and culture. From Rialto Bridge to San Marco Square...each sight is listed with pertinent information including hours and ticket prices along with a section describing ease of access. In an extensive section on music and entertainment, the author lists details of Venice's most popular concert venues, often found in basilica and palaces. A resource such as this is rare, and the author does it justice, transferring his enchantment with Venice to his reader."

—Kirkus Discoveries

"The information on transportation within Venice alone is worth the purchase price. Buy it for a friend or loved one who doesn't travel because he thinks it's too hard to get around. This book will change his mind"

—Radio Travel Producer, KPAM Portland, Oregon

"It was so easy to read, clear and detailed. I must have your book with me when I go back to Venice. The format was excellent, and can put out information you need quickly"

—Artist and long time traveler

# VENICE
## Easy Sightseeing

## A Guidebook for
## Casual Walkers, Retired Boomers
## and Wheelchair Riders

*Guida Libri per Turisti Anziani e Disabili*

## By Donald H. Bowling, M.Ed.

To get additional copies of
***Venice, Easy Sightseeing*** or ***Florence, Easy Sightseeing*** (2009),
order through www.easytravelbooks.com or www.Amazon.com.

# Contents

The location of Venice to the rest of northern Italy continues to be advantages to its attraction to travelers from Italy, Europe and around the world.

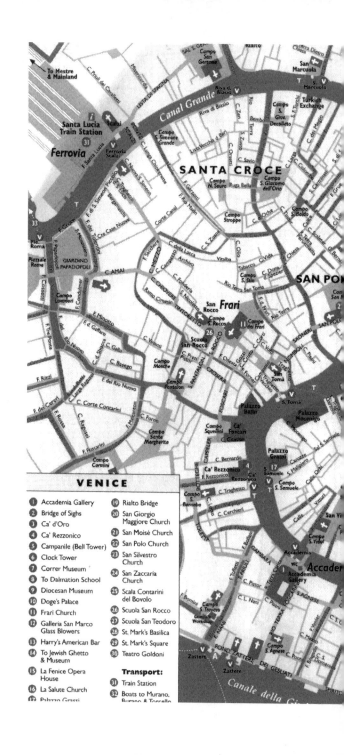

# VENICE

1. Accademia Gallery
2. Bridge of Sighs
3. Ca' d'Oro
4. Ca' Rezzonico
5. Campanile (Bell Tower)
6. Clock Tower
7. Correr Museum
8. To Dalmation School
9. Diocesan Museum
10. Doge's Palace
11. Frari Church
12. Galleria San Marco Glass Blowers
13. Harry's American Bar
14. To Jewish Ghetto & Museum
15. La Fenice Opera House
16. La Salute Church
17. Palazzo Grassi

19. Rialto Bridge
20. San Giorgio Maggiore Church
21. San Moisè Church
22. San Polo Church
23. San Silvestro Church
24. San Zaccaria Church
25. Scala Contarini del Bovolo
26. Scuola San Rocco
27. Scuola San Teodoro
28. St. Mark's Basilica
29. St. Mark's Square
30. Teatro Goldoni

**Transport:**

31. Train Station
32. Boats to Murano, Burano & Torcello

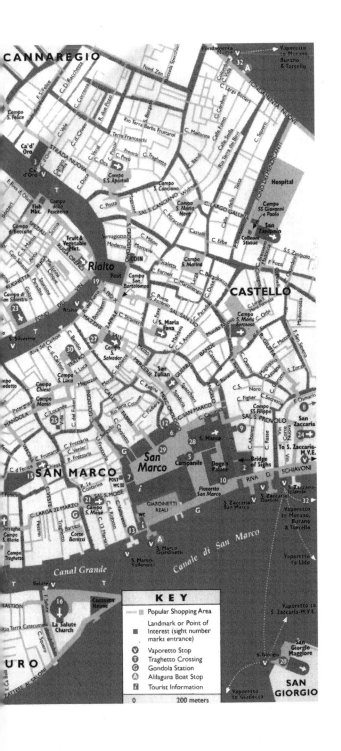

# *Introduction*

## Magnificent Venice

This unique city is overwhelming at first sight. It is so unlike anything you have ever seen or experienced. However, during the 1930s, a famous journalist wrote home to his editor: "How do you expect me to get my story, the streets are full of water!" Many Americans who get off at the train station wonder if the entire city is just boats and canals. They have reacted just as Robert Benchley did: "How am I going to see all this stuff with all this water?" A couple in Florence from Akron, Ohio who rode the train one day to Venice, told the author, "We got off the train at the station, watched the boats going up and down the Grand Canal and decided we had seen it all, and got on the train back to Florence after 45 minutes."

Approximately eighty percent of visitors stay only one day and then move on to other cities in Italy. Visitors who arrive here without planning for their trip admit they have trouble finding the famous numerous sights that this book helps you find. They can't imagine riding around in a city by boat. Some of them actually worry about getting lost.

Thankfully, this is one of the easiest cities in which to get around. The canals have water taxis, the famous gondolas, and wonderful waterbuses called the vaporetti. There are miles of beautiful alleyways that offer well-marked walking shortcuts across the many bridges of Venice. There are even special planned walkways for wheelchairs including self-operated electrical lifts at a number of bridges. They are shown at five special chapters shared by the City of Venice.

The purpose of this book is to show you how to see the beautiful sights of Venice inexpensively using the vaporetti that cruise the Grand Canal twenty-four hours per day. Enough is written about each sight so you can easily find these buildings from the docks. Almost all are within five to ten minutes from the vaporetto docks, as shown on maps showing the streets around the major Vaporetto docks on the Grand Canal. Sight guides show you the easiest way through these old structures in spite of the many stairs and missing elevators.

## Brief History

Some of the most exciting treasures on earth are in Venice, built by some of the most interesting people who changed this muddy bunch of islands into a world of marble palaces and cathedrals. The museums display hundreds of treasures brought here by the best traders of the day who sailed the Mediterranean Sea as if it were their own private lake.

How did this city become such a world power?

Thirteen centuries of Venetian history confirm that they were, as they claimed to be, the "Chosen People." They knew enough to build their world in a lagoon that protected them from the desperate hordes running loose in Italy after the fall of the Roman Empire.

They became master shipbuilders so that at one point their special shipyards would launch a ship every day of the year. Using the knowledge gained by Marco Polo, they established a monopoly on world trade to Asia. Appreciating the wisdom of other Chosen People, they invited Jews to live there. Taking advantage of Jewish knowledge of Middle Eastern culture and religious freedom of lending money, Venetians had the knowledge and money to expand their trading businesses. They invited people from the eastern Mediterranean to immigrate as laborers to expand the trading capacity of the city. Scuolas (schools) were developed by the churches to create a large population of skilled workers along with a kind of social security program for recent arrivals. When Columbus and his fellow explorers took away their world trade monopoly, they, as supreme adaptors, started another flow of wealth called **tourism.** That is probably why we all love to visit this bunch of muddy islands in Italy.

## More History Sources
If you want to dig a lot deeper into this group of formerly muddy islands, go to Google or Yahoo on a computer. Request

"Venice Italy History." Hundreds of pages are shown there. Two of the best results that I received were:

- A Brief History of Venice, Italy. (www.google.com, www.yahoo.com)
- Venice—Wikipedia, the free encyclopedia. (www.google.com, www.yahoo.com)

# *Boat, A Magic Carpet*
## The Diva of the Docks

This licensed captain operates the boat from an electronically modern, enclosed cockpit, with complete visibility of the deck and surrounding land and water.

This metal-hulled ship moves majestically through the canals and surrounding waterways, providing a safe platform for sightseeing and travel.

The best-kept secret of Venice is the bus without wheels, a neccessity to everyone who lives in Venice, and the best friend of any visitor who wants to visit the sights of Venice and not get lost. This fat, flat-bottomed bus is a powerful boat called the vaporetto. Seasoned travelers to this land of buildings that look like they are out of the Arabian Nights see these dependable waterbuses as magic carpets. These boats offer reasonably priced tickets and take you anywhere on the Grand Canal and around the islands of Venice to all of the important sights.

Over 150 of these busy, dependable people-carriers carefully pick up passengers from floating docks near many of the tourist sights. These vaporetto docks are engineered to meet boat deck levels so that passengers can easily hop on board or carefully step off. Like their land equivalent cousins, the four-wheeled bus, each bears a number, has a timetable, and has a regular route to many stops up and down the Grand Canal. Wheelchairs can roll on board whenever you see a wheelchair icon on the boat and dock.

This **Diva of the Docks** is safe, comfortable in all kinds of weather, and has a captain and conductor who help riders off and on, no matter how choppy the water. The length and width of the boat provide a very stable ride. Its width prevents a dangerous rolling and pitching when it goes into the area of the Adriatic Sea. The boat has a gentle ride that makes it possible for even the most elderly riders to walk around the deck with confidence. Passengers can be seen standing and reading newspapers. Sophisticated Italian ladies in stiletto heels seem to have no problem maintaining their balance when riding to their shopping destinations.

The vaporetto captain has radar, two-way radios, and all the necessary safety equipment to sail on canals or the open sea. Riders who become ill can get care if they have problems during their trips. You can depend on the boat to deliver its riders on a regular timetable and be the most economical way of traveling to tourist and religious sights and hotels.

This book is organized to help you use this public transportation boat to get to all the important places you need to visit in Venice. Each hotel, tourist attraction, and religious sight is matched with the appropriate vaporetto line number and dock. The book will give you step-by-step directions as well as a map of the area around the dock to find your way to the selected sights.

## Practical Information for Vaporetto Riding

Most of the time, you are on the "honor system" that exists on most European buses. However, you may have to show your ticket if the "ticket police" come on board. A friend of the author who was going to get her ticket from the deck conductor started talking and forgot. The police happened to come on board this particular day. She had to buy another kind of ticket for 50,00 euros (about $70). Her friends tease her. She is the only person they know who has gotten a ticket for a moving violation on a canal!

Avoid, if possible, Grand Canal trips during the usual commuting hours, 800 to 900 and 1600 to 1800. The boats will be very crowded during these hours with Venetians as well as tourists. You can buy your tickets from the deck conductor if the lines at the ticket booth on the dock are too long—just don't forget!

Nothing can be more discouraging than seeing a crowded vaporetto coming up to your boat dock. However, you may find space in the passenger indoor seat section, even when the boat looks full. Tourists tend to stand nervously near the exits on the open deck when they are unsure of where the boat will stop next. You are encouraged to look for a seat. The automatic voice and electronic sign call out the next stations, giving you plenty of time to exit. This guidebook also shows most of the docks in order on the Venice map. Study them just as you would city bus stops in your own hometown so you can be ready to get off.

**Cost Savings**

These boats are like an Italian city bus with most of the same rules. The tickets cost six euros for each trip and are valid for sixty minutes after you have validated them on the yellow machines at the dock.

Buy multiday travel cards at ticket offices if you plan to stay about three days. **Biglietto tre giorni** is a seventy-two-hour card that will give you a comfortable three days' use for about thirty euros. Hour-to-hour tickets will be a lot more costly and time consuming.

You could also buy **month passes** from the ticket office at Piazzale Roma. Show your passport, present a passport-sized picture and fill out a form. When you submit a completed form with 40,00 euros you will be able to buy a month's pass for 28,00 euros (you receive a receipt that acts as your pass).

This is a considerable savings from the 6,00 euros cost per trip. Passport pictures can be taken in photo booths at the train station for about 3,00 euros.

## Boat Safety in Venice

Water taxis and gondola operators are skillful boaters. However, visitors in wheelchairs cannot depend upon them to provide transportation. Wheelchair riders should depend upon the vaporetti for transportation.

Operation procedures of the vaporetti follow most safety procedures of licensed boats in the United States. Life vests and floats are readily available to passengers, with emergency procedures clearly explained in three languages and posted for your review.

## Italian Courtesy

Italian passengers and tourists from other countries all seem to adhere to the same care for fellow riders when a problem occurs. Seated riders instantly offer a seat to pregnant women, a mother with a stroller, or senior citizens. The conductor responds to the needs of a person in a wheelchair, helping the passenger enter and exit the boat. The author has even seen the captain of one of these friendly boats leave the wheelhouse to assist a passenger in a wheelchair when the water was too low for a smooth dock exit.

Trips on the vaporetti are as much fun as the sightseeing itself, as they give you a chance to see, talk to, and be a part of the Venice lifestyle.

# Finding Hidden Treasures

This massive gate was the "water gate" to the secret, naval, world-power factory of Venice.

These massive gates were the entrance to the power of Venice. The Venetian trade and ability to defend its state was centered in this eastern end of the series of islands called Venice. Around this center of power lay the twenty-four shipbuilding yards and weapon factories that made Venice the power of the Mediterranean Sea.

Vaporetti on the Grand Canal easily reach the sights of this canalled city. This book locates them by the particular vaporetto dock they are near and indicates by map where they can be found.

The map of the Grand Canal shows the docks, and the sight maps show where their particular sights are located.

**Sight Guides** provide details on the importance of the sights and touring information and indicate the difficulty of moving from the entrance to the exit.

Most of this city was built when stairs were the only method of moving from one floor to the next. Elevators are still few in number, but the Venetians take great pride in maintaining the stairs in their old buildings for safe climbing. They fortify ancient appearances by rebuilding the important support foundations and maintaining safe handrails.

### The Naval History Museum Sight Guide

The Naval History Museum Sight Guide serves as an example of the many Sight Guides that you will find in this book. This particular sight is fascinating, inexpensive, and it has some interesting challenges of which you should be aware. No elevator is available, and there are eighty-five stairs with weak handrails to climb to the third floor. The standard bathroom is on the second floor, and wheelchairs can move all over the ground floor. However, a nearby bar has a bathroom on the ground floor that the disabled can use if a companion assists them.

Look on the next page for the **Sight Guide** of the **Naval History Museum**. Do you feel like taking the 230 steps to and from the dock? What about the interior stairs? The handrails are not too sturdy. Most men, women, and children will enjoy this inexpensive museum. Many adults will be interested to see Peggy Guggenheim's private love gondola. Peggy's museum Sight Guide and her reference book, "Mistress of Modernism," will explain the significance of this boat.

The Naval History Museum is located near the entrance canal to the Arsenale Gates.

Each new sight vaporetto dock map shows the immediate area and sight locations. The following is the map of the Arsenale area that can be used to locate the appropriate trails and campos to explore the area.

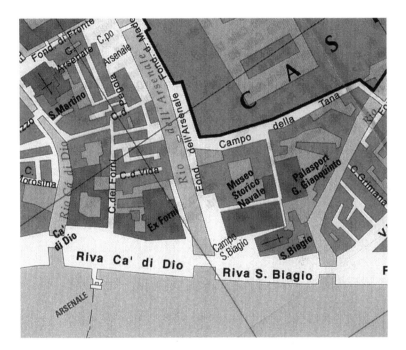

# The Naval History Museum Sight Guide

➢ **Interest**

For the navy buff, sailboat enthusiast, and boat model maker, these floors are filled with dreams. Models of Venice naval and trading ships are preserved in perfect detail.

➢ **Vaporetto Dock: Arsenal**

Boat # 1, 41, 42

➢ **Directions**

Walk twenty-five steps to the right of the dock, climb up and go down sixty wide steps over the canal bridge. There are no handrails, and it's about thirty steps to the building on the left with the large anchor near the front door.

➢ **Address**

Campo San Biagio
Castello, 2148
30122, Venezia

➢ **Admission: 1,55 euros**

➢ **Hours: 0845–1330, Monday–Saturday**

➢ **Phone: 041.510.0276**

## Ease of Touring

The building is accessible for wheelchairs only on the ground-level floor. There is no elevator and there are eighty-five steps, with poor handrails, to climb to get to the third floor. A standard restroom is located on the second floor.

## Museum Touring

This museum may be difficult touring, but is worth the effort. The building has possibly the world's best collection of ship models and real vessels from the twelfth to nineteenth century Venice. It also includes Venetian navy special war equipment, including cannons that fired stone cannonballs and fire bombs. There are also World War II one-man submarines that were used against the British Navy.

Huge Venetian ceremonial galleys, thirty to fifty feet long, will explode into view as you enter certain rooms. Some of these wooden boats have been used within the last fifty to two hundred years on the Grand Canal.

**Peggy Guggenheim's** personal gondola and two other full-sized gondolas are exhibited along with her special "love boat" of Venice.

A large-scale model of a fifteenth-century Venetian galley is on display with 138 oarsmen. These sleek ships were awesome in their battle skills with freemen instead of slaves rowing them.

Rialto Bridge was designed and built to accommodate these efficient warships.

A large model of the last Italian-built luxury liner, **The Michelangelo,** is on view. The ship sailed from 1965–1975.

You can see a huge model of a sixteenth-century Spanish galleon. It is so large that a hole was built through the next floor of the building to accommodate the masts.

**Author's Comment:** This is a treasure trove of ships and shipbuilding, and one of the most child-oriented museums in Venice. Don't miss this great bargain!

# *Music and Entertainment*

Basilicas, churches, palaces, and scuola are not only museums and places for religious services. They also serve at night as beautiful and acoustically grand concert auditoriums. Instrumental works of Vivaldi, Bach, and Handel are presented. Operatic excerpts from such operas as **La Boheme, Marriage of Figaro,** and **The Barber of Seville** can also be seen and heard all over Venice, from May through November. Hotels will also be able to provide location and times of modern music.

| Concert Hall | Vaporetto Dock | Boats |
|---|---|---|
| Chiesa S. Vidal | Accademia | 1, 82, N |
| Scuola Grande dei Carmini | Ca' Rezzonico | 1 |
| Scuola Grande di S. Giovanni Evangelista | Ferrovia (Railroad Station) | 1, 82, N |
| Teatro La Fenice Opera House | Giglio | 1 |
| Chiesa Di S. Maria Formosa | Rialto | 1, 82, N |

| Chiesa di San Giacometto (San Giacomo) | Rialto | 1, 82, N |
|---|---|---|
| Scuola Grande di San Teodoro | Rialto | 1, 82, N |
| Teatro Carlo Goldoni | Rialto | 1, 82, N |
| Teatro Malibran | Rialto | 1, 82, N |
| Ateneo di San Basso | Vallaresso/San Marco | 1, 82, N |
| Palazzo Delle Prigioni | Vallaresso/San Marco | 1, 82, N |
| Basilica dei Frari | San Toma | 1, 82, N |

www.culturalitaly.com/veniceopera.htm

Schedules for future months appear for additional major concerts and shows. An additional service will allow you to purchase tickets for concerts, plays, and operas using your credit or debit card. The number for reservations is 641.24.18029.

Don't overlook the colorful brochures in most hotels or the ones distributed on the streets of Venice. The events advertised represent the gold standard of classical music in Europe, with bargain-basement prices. During certain months of the year, there are at least ten every night of the week. The lists are constantly being expanded, and new brochures appear each month.

You can purchase tickets at your hotel, where staff members, along with this book, can help you locate the concert hall. You can also purchase tickets at the many open-door ticket areas at San Marco Square, or order through the service Hello Venezia, 041.24.24. These helpful people can provide information in English, Spanish, Italian, German, and French. You can request information about restaurants, hotels, and transportation. Of course, you can also purchase tickets at the door. A table is usually set up outside the concert hall.

All of the listed concert houses have locations, times, calendar dates, phone numbers, vaporetto docks, and additional information to help you make your selection. Concerts of comparable quality in the United States cost anywhere from $40 to $150 per seat.

Please take this opportunity to see and experience the wonderful world of Venetian music and theater. These events can truly add to your best memories of Venice.

# Chiesa S. Vidal

➢ **Vaporetto Dock: Accademia**
Boats: 1, 82, N

➢ **Directions**
Cross Accademia Bridge after leaving the stop. Walk to the first church on Campo S. Vidal.

➢ **Location**
North end of Accademia Bridge

➢ **Concerts**
Vidal, Mozart, and J.S. Bach.

➢ **Calendar**
Various dates during the year—check your brochure.

➢ **Times: Starting 2100**

➢ **Price Range: 25,00–30,00 euros**

➢ **Tickets**
Call 041.277.0561 or purchase at door. Call first to verify that a concert is scheduled.

➢ **Additional Information**
This is a large string ensemble that does not appear in costume, preferring formal attire instead. This particular former church has excellent acoustics and presents a very beautiful interior.

# *Scuola Grande del Carmini*

➤ **Vaporetto Dock: Ca' Rezzonico**
Boat: 1

➤ **Directions**
Follow the small canal called Orio di S. Barnaba at the boat dock. Turn right on Calle Pazienzea to the scuola.

➤ **Location**
Campo Santa Margherita

➤ **Concert**
Opera excerpts from Vivaldi, Mozart, Handel, and Albinoni/Calendar September December

➤ **Time: 2045**

➤ **Price: 16,00–25,00 euros**

➤ **Tickets**
Hotel, travel agency, authorized tourist guides

➤ **Additional Information**
Chamber orchestra in eighteenth-century costumes

# Scuola Grande di S. Giovanni Evangelista

➢ **Vaporetto Dock: Ferrovia (Railroad Station)**
Boat: 1, 82, N

➢ **Directions**
Cross the Scalzi bridge from the railroad station to Calle Lunga to Chioverette. Continue on Fond Gradenico to the scuola, approximately ¼ mile.

➢ **Location**
S. Polo, east of railroad station

➢ **Concerts**
Opera, ballet and excerpts from *Marriage of Figaro*, *Barber of Seville*, *Tosca*, *La Boheme*, and *La Traviata*.

➢ **Time: 2100**

➢ **Price Range: 20,00–30,00 euros**

➢ **Tickets**
Hotels and travel agencies, phone 041.522.8125

➢ **Additional Information**
The location of this scuola is out of the regular flow of tourists in Venice. However, the performances at Evangelista are varied and well worth the walk.

# Chiesa Di S. Maria Formosa

➤ **Vaporetto Dock: Rialto**
Boat: 1, 82, N

➤ **Directions**
From the boat dock, turn left on Riva del Carbon along the Grand Canal. Walk under the Rialto Bridge; turn right on C.d.F.d. Tedeschi, then turn left in front of the central post office and go on Crisostomo. Walk by Teatro Malibran and on to Calle Scaltela through Campo di S. Marna to Campo S. Formosa.

➤ **Location**
Campo Santa Maria Formosa

➤ **Concerts**
Orchestra Colegium Ducale, a Baroque orchestra plays music of Vivaldi, Corelli, Mozart, G. Rossini, and J.S. Bach.

➤ **Calendar**
September December

➤ **Time: 2100**

➤ **Price Range: 20,00–25,00 euros**

➤ **Tickets: Phone 041.984.252**

➤ **Additional Information**
This twelve-piece orchestra is a group of some of the best musicians in Venice. This orchestra also performs at the Palazzo Delle Prigioni.

# Chiesa di San Giacometto (San Giacomo)

- ➤ **Vaporetto Dock: Rialto**
  Boats: 1, 82, N

- ➤ **Directions**
  Cross Rialto Bridge to the west side and enter the church whose façade has a large clock with roman numerals.

- ➤ **Location**
  West side of the Rialto Bridge

- ➤ **Concerts**
  Rossini, Vivaldi, Mozart, Albinoni, and Handel.

- ➤ **Calendar**
  September – December

- ➤ **Time: 2045**

- ➤ **Price Range: 16,00–19,00 euros**

- ➤ **Tickets**
  Hotels and travel agencies

- ➤ **Phone: 041.426.6559**

- ➤ **Additional Information**
  Ensemble Vivaldi will play and sing compositions written by the above composers.

# Scuola Grande di San Teodoro

> ➤ **Vaporetto Dock: Rialto**
> Boats: 1, 82, N

> ➤ **Directions**
> Walk east from the bridge on Calle Larga Mazzini. Scuola is across from Chiesa San Salvador.

> ➤ **Location**
> East side of Rialto Bridge

> ➤ **Concerts**
> Opera excerpts from Rossini, Vivaldi, Offenbach, Donizetti, and Mozart.

> ➤ **Calendar**
> July - October

> ➤ **Time: 2100**

> ➤ **Price Range: 17,00–32,00 euros**

> ➤ **Tickets**
> Hotels and travel agencies

> ➤ **Additional Information**
> There may be a free concert to see across the street at **Chiesa San Salvador** after this one. But watch out for veteran concertgoers of your audience sprinting across the campo to this church!

# Basilica dei Frari

➤ **Vaporetto Dock: San Toma**
Boats: 1, 82, N

➤ **Directions**
Walk from c.d. Traghetto Vecchio to campo San Toma. Follow signs on Calle Larga and Saliz S.Rocco to the basilica.

➤ **Location**
Near Scuola San Rocco

➤ **Concerts**
Occasional religious concert music by Handel, Frank, Stadella, and Rota.

➤ **Calendar**
Concerts are irregularly scheduled; call for information.

➤ **Time: 2100**

➤ **Price Range: 8,00–12,00 euros**

➤ **Tickets: Phone 041.522.1343**

➤ **Additional Information**
Concerts are irregularly scheduled but the beauty of this Gothic cathedral makes it worth the effort to try to make the connection. It is almost the only complete Gothic-designed basilica with a wooden choir loft still in existence in Italy.

# Palazzo Delle Prigioni

➢ **Vaporetto Dock: Vallaresso**
Boat: 1, 82, N

➢ **Directions**
Turn left from the boat to the palace on the right side of the Bridge of Sighs.

➢ **Location**
Near the Bridge of Sighs

➢ **Concerts**
Vivaldi, Rossini, Schubert and Corelli.

➢ **Calendar**
November and December

➢ **Time: 2100**

➢ **Price Range: 20,00–25,00 euros**

➢ **Tickets: Phone 041.984.252**

➢ **Additional Information**
The ensemble is prepared to play a repertoire ranging from the Baroque to twenty-first century music.

**The Palazzo Delle Prigioni**, linked to the Doge's Palace by the **Bridge of Sighs,** is the opera house by sixteenth-century architect **Antonio da Ponte**. The building was destined to substitute partially for the cells of the Doge's Palace. Since 1922, by the will of **Prince Umberto of Savoia,** the Prisons of the Doge's Palace are the headquarters of the prestigious **Artistic Circle of Venice,** and some of the most important musicians played here. Every year the Artistic Circle puts on exhibitions and other displays that are in public demand, such as **Biennale di Arte e di Architettura Moderna di Venezia.** It is possible to tour this building before the concert.

# *Ateneo di San Basso*

➢ **Vaporetto Dock: Vallaresso**
Boats: 1, 82, N

➢ **Directions**
Facing the basilica turn left and walk past the stone lions to Calle San Basso.

➢ **Location**
San Marco Square

➢ **Concerts**
Tributes to Vivaldi and Mozart

➢ **Calendar**
July–October

➢ **Time: 2030**

➢ **Price Range: 20,00–25,00 euros**

➢ **Tickets**
Hotels or the two ticket agencies at San Marco Square

➢ **Phone: 041.538.825**

➢ **Additional Information**
The programs alternate between opera and instrumentals.

The orchestra **Virtuosi di Venezia-San Marco Chamber Orchestra** reproduces in its concerts the atmosphere and the genius of **Vivaldi** compositions. The ensemble and the musical formation have been chosen to recall the exact situation in which Vivaldi worked. Even the decision to perform in the prestigious **Ateneo di San Basso in San Marco Square** follows this tradition.

It has the same dimensions as the **Pieta Institute** music hall in which Vivaldi composed.

# *Teatro Malibran*

➤ **Vaporetto Dock: Rialto**
Boat: 1, 82, N

➤ **Directions**
From Rialto dock, travel north across the near end of the Rialto Bridge from the vaporetto dock to c.d.f.d. Tedeschi. Turn right and then left on s.d. Font. c.d.f.d. Tedeschi. Cross a small canal bridge and continue on Crisostomo to the church and turn right. Watch for a large Teatro Malibran sign.

➤ **Location**
North of Rialto Bridge, past Venice's central post office

➤ **Concerts**
Malibran is both an opera house and theater. The authors saw a very famous comic opera, *The SecretMarriage* by Domenico Cimarosa. The quality of this opera with its full orchestra and large cast was as good as any seen in New York or San Francisco. Recitals of Bach, Beethoven, Debussy, Brahms, Sibelius, Grieg, Schubert, Ravel, Haydn, and Zemblinsky are also conducted.

➤ **Calendar**
September 27–May 12

➤ **Time: 2030**

➤ **Price Range: 50,00–125,00 euros (opera prices)**

> **Tickets**
  Hotels, Vivaldi Ticket Agency

> **Phone: 041.78.6511**

> **Additional Information**
  This teatro is an affiliate of the famous La Fenice Opera
  House. Information regarding performances can be obtained
  for both theaters and translated at **www.hellovenezia.com**

The production of a historical drama during Carnavale reflects
the variety of stage plays at Venetian theaters.

# Teatro Carlo Goldoni

➢ **Vaporetto Dock: Rialto**
Boats: 1, 82, N

➢ **Directions**
From the square, turn left at c.d. Forno, and the theater will be a short block from that turn.

➢ **Location**
Walk along the canal from the boat dock toward San Marco Square.

➢ **Performances**
Classic and modern plays

➢ **Calendar**
All year

➢ **Time**
Box office 1000–1300, Monday–Saturday; performances 1500–1900, Monday–Saturday

➢ **Price Range: 20,00–80,00 euros**

➢ **Tickets: Phone 041.240.2011**

➢ **Additional Information**
Wheelchair accessible

# Teatro La Fenice

➢ **Vaporetto Dock: Giglio**
Boat: 1

➢ **Directions**
Walk from the dock down a long narrow passageway, Calle Gritti o del back Maria Zobenigo. This street deadends at a canal. Look to your right, and you will see the La Fenice Opera House. Keeping the opera house in your sight, take the walkways to the left around another building to the front.

➢ **Location**
Near Campo Maria Zobenigo

➢ **Performances**
Operas and vocal concerts

➢ **Calendar**
All year

➢ **Price Range: From 20,00–100,00 euros**
Depending on seat location and the production

➢ **Tickets**
Vivaldi Box Office Stores

➢ **Phone: 041.984.252**

➢ **Additional Information**
This is a magnificent building and has a wonderful history. See **La Fenice, Rebuilding a Legend,** at the sight description.

# Vivaldi, the Venice Music Legend

Vivaldi is on almost every concert program in Venice's high season, between May and October. In fact, this former priest's music is almost synonymous with the city. It can be heard in perhaps two or three concerts each night.

**Antonio Vivaldi** was born in Venice in 1678. Though ordained a priest in 1703, according to his own account, Vivaldi no longer wished to celebrate mass. A "tightness of chest" prevented him from performing this important function. Present medical knowledge determines that he may have had asthmatic bronchitis.

He wrote many fine and memorable concertos, such as the **Four Seasons** and **Opus #3.**

The **Ospedale delle Pieta** employed Vivaldi for most of his working life. Often termed an "orphanage/hospital," this Ospedale was in fact a home for female children of noblemen not married to the girl's mothers. The Ospedale was thus well financed by the "anonymous" fathers. Its furnishings were opulent. The young women were well looked after, and the musical education and standards were among the highest in Venice. Many Vivaldi concerts were performances in which he would accompany his many talented pupils.

Vivaldi's relationship with the Ospedale began right after his ordination in 1703, when he was named as a violin teacher there. Until 1709, Vivaldi's appointment was renewed every year and again after 1711. Between 1709 and 1711, Vivaldi was not attached to the Ospedale. Perhaps in this period he was already working for the **Teatro Sant' Angelo,** an opera theater.

In 1713, Vivaldi took a leave from the Ospedale della Pieta in order to stage his first opera, **Ottone in Villa.** In the 1713–1714 season, he worked again for the Teatro Sant' Angelo, where he produced other operas.

At the end of 1717, Vivaldi moved to **Mantua** for two years in order to take up his post as **chamber kapellmeister**. His task there was to provide operas, cantatas, and perhaps concert music as well. His opera *Armada* had already been performed earlier in Mantua, and in 1719, *Teuzzone* and *Tito Manlio* followed. A note at the bottom of his score, "Music by Vivaldi, Made in Five Days," demonstrates the speed of his composing.

In 1720, Vivaldi returned to Venice where he again staged new operas that he wrote in the Teatro Sant'Angelo. In Mantua, he had made the acquaintance of the singer **Anna Giraud,** and she moved in to live with him. Vivaldi maintained that she was no more than a housekeeper and good friend.

Earlier, in the 1660s, musical life in **Rome** had been enormously stimulated by the presence of a Catholic convert queen, **Christina of Sweden**. A few years later, she moved to Rome and took up residence in the **Palazzo Riario.** There she organized musical events that were attended by composers such as **Corelli** and **Scarlatti**. Like them, Vivaldi moved there and profited from the favorable cultural climate in the city.

Despite his stay in **Rome,** Vivaldi remained in the service of the Ospedale delle Pieta. He was required only to send two concertos per month to Venice, for which he received money. His presence was never required. He also remained director of the Teatro Sant'Angelo from 1726 to 1728.

Between 1725 and 1728, some eight operas premiered in Venice and Florence. **Abbot Conti** wrote of his contemporary, Vivaldi: "In less than three months Vivaldi has composed three operas, two for Venice and a third for Florence; the last has given something of a boost to the name of the theater of that city.

During these years, Vivaldi was also extremely active in the field of concertos. In 1726, he published a sequence of concertos in **Amsterdam**. This consisted of twelve concertos, seven of which were descriptive: **The Four Seasons, Storm at Sea, Pleasure,** and **The Hunt.** These concertos were enormously successful, particularly in **France.**

In 1738, Vivaldi was in **Amsterdam** where he conducted at the **Schouwburg Theater.** Returning to Venice in 1740, he was later invited to Vienna. His stay in Vienna was to be brief, however. He died July 28, 1741, "of internal fire" (probably the asthmatic bronchitis from which he suffered all of his life), and, like **Mozart** fifty years later, he received a modest burial. **Anna Giraud**, his lifelong companion, returned to Venice, where she died in 1750.

# Sights Are Arranged by Vaporetto Docks

Vaporetto Boat #1 is like a local bus on the Grand Canal, with # 82 running like an express bus, only stopping at the most popular docks.

You will find the many sights in this guidebook to be no more than a five- to fifteen-minute walk from the vaporetto boat docks on the waterways. Each place has been located on a map, described in detail, and explained in terms of steps and easiest access.

These docks are not arranged in the order they appear on the Grand Canal. Instead, they are arranged in order of general interest. The most popular visiting places are introduced to you early on the Grand Canal to remind you to start early at the most crowded places as San Marco, Rialto, and Ca' Rezzonico. Others are shown in an order to encourage your visit throughout the rest of the day. Let's assume that your starting place is Ferrovia, the vaporetto docks at the train station. Using the information that you have learned about riding these boat buses, board a boat #82 or #1 and start up the Grand Canal.

# San Marco Vallaresso Dock— Pigeons by Day, Dancing at Night

➢ **Vaporetto Dock: Vallaresso San Marco**
Boats: 1, 82, N

➢ **Sights**
San Marco Square, Basilica S. Marco
Campanile S. Marco
Palazzo Ducale
Museo Civic Correr
Chiesa San Moise
Bridge of Sighs

➢ **Concerts**
Ateneo San Basso

A magnificent bell tower with an elevator to the top; the Doge Palace to the right joined to a "classical prison" by the so-called Bridge of Sighs presents a famous skyline.

The most impressive entrance to San Marco Square leads visitors through two historic pillars by the bell tower on the left and the Doge Palace on the right.

A busy foot-bridge with the Bridge of Sighs in the background.

The gold-filled San Marco Basilica that contains great wealth and plunder from the Fourth Crusade in Constantinople.

# San Marco Square

➢ **Interest**

Sights are available galore during the day. At night, four orchestras start playing alternatively from about 7:00 p.m. The magic of a summer's night transforms this huge rectangle to an oversized nightclub.

➢ **Vaporetto Dock: Vallaresso San Marco**

Boats: 1, 82, N

➢ **Directions**

Walk to the right from the boat dock about about 250 yards through a small park and turn left through the two large granite pillars. Behold, this was called the Drawing Room of Europe by Napoleon.

**Ease of Touring**

During the day, this square is crowded with tourists who come to see the **Bell Tower, Doge's Palace**, and **San Marco Basilica**. You should be aware that it is very crowded between the hours of 1000–1800. Be sure to view the square in the evening to experience its beauty. It becomes a giant nightclub with orchestras competing for your attention.

If you are willing to spend approximately thirty euros, you can sit and have wine or coffee at a table. You could stand at the back of the table and chair area and enjoy the same music free, but with no food or drink. If you haven't had dinner eating there could be a very memorable experience, though it may be a little pricey.

The charm of the evening includes the sparkling silhouette of the basilica and the huge U-shaped building with its shops and bars all facing the square. Dancing is welcomed, and all ages participate.

If you travel during the night, the #N vaporetto offers frequent and safe transportation.

**Author's Comments:** If this square looks familiar to you, it should. It has appeared in a number of Hollywood films. Film buff trivia question: how many can you name? Remember, this is the one place everyone who has ever been to Venice will ask about: "Did you see **San Marco?**"

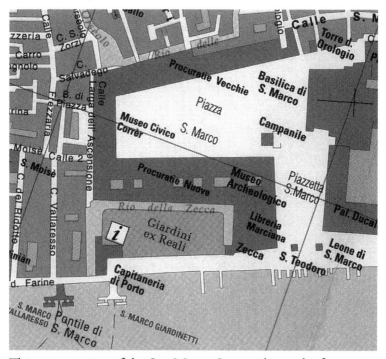

This pigeon view of the San Marco Square shows the five major sights that can be visited when walking from the Vallaresso Vaporetto Dock.

# *Campanile*
## San Marco Bell Tower and the Lion of St. Marks & St. Theodore

➢ **Interest**

Go to the top and use your camera for great pictures of San Marco Square, and get some spectacular views of Venice and surrounding islands.

➢ **Vaporetto Dock: Vallaresso San Marco**

Boats 1, 82, N

➢ **Directions**

Turn right from the boat dock. Walk about 250 yards over two canal bridges, past a well-maintained park with bathrooms, and a number of vendors. Walk between two large granite pillars, look up, and there you are!

➢ **Location**

San Marco Square

➢ **Admission: 6,00 euros**

➢ **Hours**

0930–Sunset, April–September
0930–1600, November–March

## Ease of Touring

An elevator will take you to the top after a few steps from the
ground level.

## Tower History

Started originally in 888 CE, this tower is still the tallest
building in Venice. It was once a lighthouse as well as a bell
tower. In 1902, it imploded into a pile of bricks; no one was
hurt but the lighthouse keeper's cat reportedly disappeared.

Before this destruction, an Austrian conqueror's claim to fame
was that he, **Duke Frederick II,** rode up the thirty-seven flights
of stairs atop his horse. **Galileo** reportedly climbed up to the
bells with his telescope to view heavenly bodies.

The tenacity of the Venetians in rebuilding this landmark is
demonstrated by the following list of materials required to
complete it after ten years of work: 1,204,000 bricks, 11,860
tons of concrete, 4 tons of iron for the reinforced concrete,
6.23 tons of iron for the belfry, and 4.5 tons of copper. Keep
in mind that all of this material traveled to the site by way of
barges on the Grand Canal.

The present bell tower is considered safe enough to carry
thousands of tourists to the top in an elevator every day.

## The Lion of St. Marks & St. Theodore

The two fine granite columns you walked between to get to the bell tower arrived from Egypt in the twelfth century and were placed at the entrance to San Marco Square as a symbol of Venetian justice.

Workers placed the winged lion of St. Mark at the top of the column nearest the Palazzo Ducale. They placed the statue of St. Theodore, fourth century, on the other. Public executions took place between these two columns. This also gave Venetian mothers a place to point to when they had misbehaving children.

Until the sixteenth century, people also used the campanile for public ridicule. Officials suspended several priests in gabbias (cages). They had to endure public ridicule hanging from a pole in a small cage. According to records, they received only bread and water for up to two months for blasphemy. That also gave mothers something to point at.

**Author's Comments**: Try not to be at the top of the tower at noon! Note the lion on the top of the pillar. He is standing alone. Most of the lions you see in Venice have a book in front of them with a paw holding it in place. The position of this book is to signify openness.

# Doge Palace
## Palazzo Ducale and Palace of the Grand Duke

➢ **Interest**
This building is a combination of The White House, Supreme Court and Congress of the old Republic of Venice. It even had its own dungeons. Many political and diplomatic battles were fought in this building. Venice was a country that did not want their doge to get too much power. He was surrounded by a myriad of checks and balances that could lead to his execution if he departed from the wishes of the majority.

➢ **Vaporetto Dock: Vallaresso San Marco**
Boat: 1, 82, N

➢ **Directions**
Walk to the right of the dock. Pass the park and cross the bridge past the two marble columns. The entrance to the ticket office is to your left.

➢ **Address**
Palazzo Ducale, 2, San Marco Square

➢ **Admission: 13,00 euros**

➢ **Phone: 041.522.4951**

➢ **Hours**
0900–1730 Daily April–October, 0900–1530 Daily November–March

## Ease of Touring

Wheelchair accessible. When purchasing tickets, you may want to notify the staff about your need to use an elevator.

## Special Tours

Interrogation rooms for prisoners and secret passageways tours can be taken if you call the phone number 041.522.4951 prior to arriving. Enhance your tour of this palace by buying the book *Doge's Palace in Venice.*

Bathrooms are located off the staircase on the far right, on the ground floor and the loggia floor of the palace.

## Palace History

The **Doge's Palace** is a masterpiece of **Gothic artistry** of the fourteenth and fifteenth centuries. This emblem of the **Republic of Venice** is an unusual combination of airy light galleries and arcades supporting a heavy upper structure. This building has a huge courtyard and many rooms that housed a government of a special empire. It demonstrates the broad effect this city-state had upon the world.

The present structure covers up a fortress-like design, included when construction began in 814 CE. Moats, drawbridges, and corner towers were eventually removed. The reconstruction in 1173 gave the building a **Byzantine** appearance. This structure eventually changed with present facades acquiring more of the

**Arabian Nights** look of the **basilica**. This seat of government reflects the riches of Venice during its peak of world influence during the fifteenth, sixteenth, and seventeenth centuries.

Touring the present interiors provides a grand lesson through viewing huge paintings by **Titian, Tintoretto, Veronese, Jacopo Palma il Giovane,** and **Jacopo Bassano**. One floor contains the **Doge's** apartments and the huge meeting room, **Sala del Maggior Consiglio,** with room for 2,622 members of a sort of special **Venetian parliament**. A large armory on the second floor shows the military weapons that probably kept the Venetians winning battles against other city-states for many years. Other rooms contained space for the government and Venice's unique kind of justice.

A partially hidden door between the basilica and the Palazzo Ducal in the courtyard best demonstrates the unusual Venetian relationship between church and state. It also hints of the basilica's formal role as **Chapel to the Doge.**

**Napoleon's** rule and later control by Austria did not destroy Venice's ability to maintain their government, even after removal of the Doge's position. The unification of Italy in the nineteenth century left the present **Palazzo Ducale** as a beautiful collection of art and a center of memories of the way that this city-state was ruled.

In general, the following shows how to plan your tour if you prefer the top-down touring method. Ride the elevator to the third floor to start your movement down the steps.

**Third Floor: Sala dell' Anticolloquio** (foreign ambassador's reception rooms)

These are rooms of the State Security and Council of Ten (described more completely on the next page) and rooms for interrogating prisoners.

**Second Floor: The Doge's Apartments**
The Doge's "West Wing," Sala Del Maggior Consiglio (Grand Council chambers) and armory.

**First Floor: Sala del Maggior Consiglio** (law offices)
Offices for the chancellor, the censors, and offices of the navy.

**Ground Floor**
Entrance, courtyard and exit to San Marco Square.

**Loggia Floor**
Chambers of the government censors, military offices, and entrance to the prison and **Bridge of Sighs**.

**Ground Floor**
Museo dell'Opera, courtyard, exit to **San Marco Square** and the **Basilica** through the garden.

**Authors Comment:** You should visit the **Bridge of Sighs** and walk down to the area where the prisoners were kept. Step inside one of the cells to get a feeling of what some citizens of Venice experienced in the "Serene Republic." It will also show the motivating force that drove Casanova to escape.

# 🖋 Venice's Remarkable Government

The first island settlements began in the seventh century and grew into a single government for purposes of defense, welfare, and trade. They created a sort of dukedom under the leadership of someone with the title **Doge** (grand duke). These doges developed their leadership roles to a grand level as the city-state of Venice grew grander.

The monopoly of trade, after the journeys of Marco Polo and ongoing successes in trade and warfare, made Venice one of the most powerful countries on earth. The role of the doge became more and more regal and powerful. However, the traditional Italian desire for representative government developed a series of checks and balances to keep the doges working for the good of the city-state. One hundred twenty-five doges existed from 697 to 1797, with a democratic government keeping them honest and responsible to the people.

Something likened to a combined **Supreme Court** and **prison system existed** in two offices called the **State Security** and **Council of Ten**. If you view the Council of Ten's meeting chamber today you can find a place where unsigned notes, accusing citizens of treason, could be privately stuck in a box that would be read by the Council.

Unsigned notes were also placed in a series of lion-headed "mail boxes" located around the city of Venice. These also were delivered to the Council of Ten and might lead to the arrest of a citizen of Venice, unsigned.

If the council believed this evidence, the accused would be arrested, brought in for "trial" and taken next door to the prison on the **Bridge of Sighs** for possible torture and imprisonment. This bridge got its name usually because it is where the prisoners had their last view of the outside world. Family and loved ones would stand outside and cry their names and call to them as they were being taken away.

As a tourist, you need only stand in these rooms and walk across the **Bridge of Sighs** for a taste of Venetian justice. The island country of Venice exhibited a strong paranoia toward traitors, who could give away trade secrets. If you think about the nature of a small nation that is constantly under the threat of attack, you can see why this sort of justice existed.

# San Marco Basilica

> ### Interest
> See a church of gold. Bright lights are turned on inside each day at 1100. You will feel like you are in a golden nugget. Walk up the stairs and view the magnificent, world-famous horses as you use the opportunity to take memorable photographs from the outside balcony.

> ### Vaporetto Dock: San Marco
> Vallaresso, Boats 1, 82, N

> ### Directions
> Walk about a hundred yards past the bell tower and turn right.

> ### Location
> San Marco Basilica, Piazza San Marco

> ### Admission
> The Basilica floor is free. **Pay 3,00 euros** to climb stairs or ride an elevator, where you can view the original Four Horses from Constantinople. Walk out onto the balcony overlooking the square—copies of these gold and bronze originals are outside. **For 2,10 euros**, you can see the Chancel & Pala d'Oro.

> ### Hours
> 0945–1700 Monday–Saturday; 1400–1600 Sunday

> ### Note
> Try to be at the basilica before opening time. The lines grow quite long and start very early.

## Ease of Touring

Wheelchairs can enter the basilica through the left entrance. There is a small step inside the entrance. At the front entrance, a sign instructs visitors to check any luggage they have before entering. Cameras can be carried as long as they are not used in the interior.

The forty-two-step climb to the top leads to an outdoor walkway around the upper part of the façade. The ground marble floor has no obstructions. Contact the museum personnel, as there is an elevator to the second floor and two platform lifts that make the route entirely accessible.

## Basilica Touring

The **Basilica** of **San Marco** is one of the most valuable churches in the world. It is home to over 4,000 square feet of mosaic artwork, covering the interior with rubies, diamonds, emeralds, precious marbles, and gold. No expense was spared in the creating this final resting place for **Saint Mark.**

The present San Marco Basilica was constructed in 1094. The architect is unknown; however, the design is considered **Greek-Byzantine** with **Arab, Lombard,** and **Germanic** influences.

Later generations continued to add extensions and decorate the original church. Marble and golden mosaic decorative coverings add to the sparkling gold interior seen today.

**San Marco Basilica** looks like something out of the **Arabian Nights** compared to other Italian cathedrals. Five domes were added in 1100 and the interior was covered with mosaics. There are scenes from the Bible with gold mosaic backgrounds.

The doges of Venice used this basilica as their private chapel. In addition, Venetians came to the basilica to "crown" each doge, start crusades to the Holy Land, surrender to **Napoleon**, and eventually declare the city independent from **Austria** and **France.**

## Museum Quattro Cavalli
## The Four Horses

The original bronze and gold horses are kept indoors. They are one of the most valuable art pieces captured in the fourth crusade now seen at the Basilica.

Again, they come from Constantinople, where they stood above the **Hippodrome**, advertising a great day at the races. No one is entirely sure of the origins of these bronze and gold horses. For many years, they were attributed to a **Greek** sculptor of the fourth century BCE, but the idea has recently emerged that they may be an original **Roman** work of the second century CE.

They are the only quadrigae (four-house chariots) to have survived from classical times, and their triumphal positions, at the front of the basilica, have symbolized Venice's power. **Napoleon** couldn't resist taking them and installing them on the **Arc of Triumph** in Paris, but his luck ran out at **Waterloo**. The horses were returned to Venice, where they have remained for the entire world to enjoy. Eventually copies were placed outside to preserve the original horses, which still reside inside the basilica.

## The Chancel and Pala d'Oro

Back on the main floor, you will find flat, smooth marble with special entrances to golden altarpieces. Access to Pala d'Oro altarpieces involves four quite steep steps. This altar screen is one of the richest in the world. It is covered by more than 3,000 precious stones and enamel icons inlaid in gold.

The treasury is in a side room with two relatively low steps at the entrance, one step on the right, and one on the left inside the room.

Most of the gold, jewels, and special marble of the Basilica were brought back to Venice by the Fourth Crusade to create a new capital of trade in the Mediterranean.

## Baptistery and Zen Chapel

This contains the Gothic tomb of Doge Andrea Dandolo and some interesting mosaics, including one of Salome dancing. Unfortunately, this chapel has long been closed. Special permission is needed to visit it and the adjoining Zen Chapel, with its bronze tomb of Cardinal Zen. The phone number to call for its visitation is 041.533.5303.

**Author's Comments:** This cathedral is one of the best symbols of the wealth and power of Venice at its peak in history

# Correr Museum

➢ **Interest**

This museum displays one of the most extensive art and history collection of Venice. On a warm day, it's air conditioning and lovely padded benches preserve the energy of even the most wearied visitor.

➢ **Vaporetto Dock: Vallaresso San Marco**

Boats: 1, 82, N

➢ **Directions**

Walk down Calle Vallaresso about 200 yards after leaving the boat dock. Turn right on Calle San Moise and proceed fifty yards to the entrance of San Marco Square. Turn left and move about fifty yards to the entrance of the museum. The entrance to this huge exhibit is opposite the San Marco Basilica in San Marco Square. Stairs or a lift from the ground floor can reach the thirty-one rooms of the first floor.

➢ **Location**

San Marco Square

➢ **Admission: 13,00 euros**

➢ **Phone: 04.522.5625**

➢ **Hours**

April–October 900–1900 / November–March 900–1700

## Ease of Touring

In reality, the Correr Museum is three museums connected together on the first and second floors of much of the building surrounding the square. A huge set of forty-five white stone stairs, built for Napoleon, provides a grand entrance but can also be a barrier to seniors and wheelchair tourists. The entrance to bypass the large staircase is on Calle del Salvadego. You can make arrangements by telephone at 041.240.5211 or have a party member go up to the ticket office on the first floor to request that a staff member bring the elevator down for the person needing assistance. This is easier than it sounds; staff personnel are more than happy to accommodate your request.

## Museum Touring

Museo Correr is one of the more comfortable places to visit in San Marco Square. It is cool all year long and filled with comfortable chairs and padded benches in the center of each exhibit room. It has a fine cafeteria and a huge collection of art and old photographs to enjoy.

You can see an institutional history of the city in the centuries of its greatness and political independence. A collection of small renaissance bronzes from the fifteenth and sixteenth centuries is shown with this same collection.

The museum proper begins with neoclassical palace rooms on the first floor. It has twenty-eight rooms filled with sculptures by **Antonio Canova,** Napoleon's favorite. The history of Venice is traced from its humble beginnings to the more complex story with the recent European invasions by France, Austria, Germany, and, of course, the last invasion world tourism.

Stairs or a lift from the first floor can reach the thirty-one rooms of the second floor.

The second floor contains Venetian **Byzantine** art, decorated international Gothic art, Flemish and German painters' work, and the work of the **Bernini** family. A remarkable collection of ivory from **Roman, Gothic,** and the **Renaissance** periods is well exhibited. Paintings, objects, and important documents of the events in Venice show the **"Risorgimento Period"** from the end of the Republic through the **French** and **Austrian** domination, and through the annexation of the Kingdom of Italy. The patriotic works of **Danielle Manin** are the centerpiece of the **Risorgimento Museum.**

Venetian nobleman **Teodoro Correr**, 1750–1830, collected much of the contents of these rooms. They began to be assembled, added to, and exhibited in several palaces on the Grand Canal. Eventually, they were placed in the present regal setting in 1922.

**Author's Comments:** This is one of the few musems that will give you the complete picture of the origin and development of this famous city.

# Chiesa S Moise

> **Interest**
>
> There is a gondola station on this minor canal. You can stand on the bridge and watch "gondola rush hour," complete with singers, accordion players, and, of course, tourists. There is a variety of excellent upscale shops, theaters, restaurants, and places to sit and enjoy Venice.

> **Vaporetto Dock: Vallaresso San Marco**
>
> Boat: 1, 82, N

> **Directions**
>
> You may see one unique facade among Venetian churches by walking down Calle Vallaresso to Sal da S. Moise and walking left on Campo San Moise, by the famous **Harry's Bar.**

> **Address**
>
> Campo San Moise

> **Admission: Free**

> **Phone: 041.5285840**

> **Hours**
>
> 0930–1230 Daily

## Ease of Touring

The main entrance has an eight-inch step, and the secondary entrance has a very small step to go to the interior.

## Church Touring

Venetians believe the foundation of this parochial church is the oldest in the city: 1,200 years. The church was dedicated to Moses and suffered a number of fires. Alexander Tremignon built the present Baroque façade after one of the fires.

This church façade shows statues of camels made by someone who seems to have never seen one. Cupids, angels, and saints make up the base example of early Renaissance. If you have young children, this façade has the look of a Dr. Seuss book and could certainly entertain them while the rest of you are touring the interior.

The **Baroque** interior is bursting with works of art including busts of the **Fini** family, **Tintoretto's la Lavanda dei Piedi** and an image of Christ washing his disciples' feet, to the left of the high altar.

**Author's Comment:** This is another church that John Ruskin, the architect critic (1819–1900), stated was "notable as one of the basest examples of the basest school of the Renaissance in Venice for its manifestation of insolent atheism." His book, *The Stones of Venice*, made it clear that in his opinion, only Gothic churches were truly Christian.

# *Rialto Dock—Center of Venice*

➢ **Vaporetto Dock: Rialto**
Boats: 1, 82, N

➢ **Sights**
Rialto Bridge Area
Walk on South Side of SM Formosa
Easy Walk to the Snail

➢ **Concerts**
Teatro Malibran
Teatro Goldoni
Scuola Grande di San Teodoro
Church of San Giacomo

The Rialto Bridge can be seen connecting the commercial center of Rialto with its Vaporetto Docks on the right and its boat mooring on the left.

This is the "Snail" spiral staircase of the Contarini del Bovolo Palace built when Columbus was crossing the Atlantic Ocean.

Santa Maria Formosa Church houses tributes to Saint Barbara and the painting of the Venetian Renaissance Woman Giulia Lama.

# *Rialto Bridge*

➢ **Interest**

The unique bridge in this area began as a number of boats tied together. Two or three wooden bridges later, this remarkable stone bridge was built by a man who beat Michelangelo in the contest for its design. This bridge symbolizes the flamboyance, cleverness, and enterprise of this extraordinary city of Venice.

➢ **Vaporetto Dock: Rialto Southside of the Bridge**

Boats: 1, 82, N

➢ **Location**

Five vaporetto docks north of the railroad station. Nine vaporetto docks south of San Marco Dock. The center of everything!

This high point of land became the first original city center of Venice. It was a prime location because the height offered one of the few places where buildings would not be flooded when the water rose. Ferries, gondolas, and workboats provided movement from one side of the Grand Canal to the other. Galley ships were able to pass beneath this first stone bridge with its high arch, built in 1591.

**Tour of the Northwest Side of the Bridge**

This area has a huge market and tourist business area. It leads one about one-third of a mile by alleyways to a large Campo named San Polo. Other alleyways lead about another two-thirds of a mile to the grand Basilica Frari and eventually Piazzale Roma and eventually Piazzale Roma at about 1.3 miles away from Rialto with its car garages near the train station.

This map of the Rialto area shows the location of its more important sights.

Another alleyway takes visitors by the fifteenth-century church, San Giacomo di Rialto, the market area and a circle of restaurants and bars. San Giacomo dell' Orio church, with a roof constructed by boat builders, is about two-thirds of a mile away. This Venetian family campo with shops and apartments leads onto the Scalzi Bridge and the railroad station about one and a half miles away from the Rialto Bridge.

If you feel energetic enough to try to follow these walks, be prepared for an hour or so of interesting shopping to each destination. Watch for **Ferrovia Railroad Station** or **San Polo** written on buildings for your directions for these two walks. Do not be shy to ask shop owners for directions.

### The Rialto Bridge

Kiss your partner when you reach the top of this old stone bridge. All the television ads show this happening in the center of San Marco. However, a longer tradition says this is the place to show your affection. If it is a hot day, this is supposed to be the coolest place in the area. Crowds tend to move up and down the bridge by the shops located in the center of the bridge. If you want to bypass the crowds, use the outside railing area.

### Wheelchairs

Visitors in wheelchairs should avoid the Rialto Bridge. Its builders were not aware of developmental disability standards in their time two hundred years before the voyages of Columbus.

The **Accessibility Map on Rialto** shows that it is best to visit the area near the Rialto vaporetto dock where most of the sights and theaters are located. To visit the other side of the bridge, take the vaporetto one stop toward San Marco and get off at San Silvestro Dock. Take Calle S. Silvestro on the right side of the dock the short distance to Ruga VF. Giovanni and go to the right. You will be able to enjoy the exciting markets and see the oldest church in Venice with its huge clock, San Giacomo di Rialto.

### Chiesa di San Giacometto San Giacomo

This small church is known for its large clock that is usually correct one or two times a day. The beauty of the church is inside. Planned as a Greek cross design, its original Greek marble columns survive complete with Venetian-Byzantine tops and organic decorations.

On the left is an altar by **Scamozzi,** 1553–1616, along with bronzes by **Gerolamo Campagna,** 1550–1620. On the right is an **Annunciation** by **Marco Vecellio,** 1545–1611, who was a cousin of **Titian.** Information about concerts held here appears in the Entertainment section of this book.

### Mercato di Rialto

The market area in front of this old church can sometimes seem like a day on the best rides at Disneyland. The last time I visited this wonderful place, a cacophony of sounds, smells, and wild sights greeted me at this large ensemble of brilliantly colored fruits and vegetables grown at the market garden island of Sant' Erasmo.

Loud farmers and fishmongers sold the fruits, vegetables, poultry, meats, and seafood and presided over cases of unusual-looking fish and things I hope are not in the water when I swim in the ocean. Just when I became used to the din, someone shouted, "Anguilla!" and several women began screaming. A four-foot eel was making his break for freedom. A market man quickly scooped up the escaping snake-like fish. Things returned to a busy shopping experience, with the unfortunate eel going back to being someone's dinner. This is one of the best shows in town and there is no admission charge!

This market area becomes a giant flea market on Sundays with the Venetians bringing out all the usual things of garage-sale quality. The only difference between their garage sales and ours is that when we take their things home with us, they become prizes from Venice, Italy.

# Chiesa Santa Maria Formosa

## ➢ Interest

One of the first churches in Venice seems to have been especially blessed by women. A bishop from Orderzo had a vision of an extremely attractive (Formosan) Virgin Mary asking him to build a church wherever he saw a white cloud touch the ground. **Saint Barbara**, the 1598 patron saint of Venetian artillerymen, had a chapel built in her honor. There are several statues placed outside the church also. This church also has a painting by one of the few recognized Venetian women artists of sixteenth-century Venice, Giulia Lama.

## ➢ Vaporetto Dock: Rialto

Boats: 1, 82, N
Gondola: This church may also be reached by riding one of the many gondolas available.

## ➢ Directions

Walk toward the **Rialto Bridge** from either vaporetto dock. Climb ten steps and turn right on Salizada Pio X Street. Walk to **S. Bartolomeo Campo** and walk on the left side of the statue of **Goldoni.** Walk to the canal bridge by the **Coin Department Store.** Walk to a church and turn right. You will see the **Teatro Malibran** sign. Walk to the right of the theater, turn right, and go over the small canal bridge. Continue on to **Campo S. Marino.** Take Pindemonte over two canal bridges to **Campo Formosa.** This is about a twenty-minute walk if you take time to window shop.

➢ **Location**
Campo Santa Maria Formosa Castello

➢ **Admission: 2,50 euros**

➢ **Phone: 041.275.0642 or 041.523.4645 or 041.984252**

➢ **Hours**
1000–1700 Monday–Saturday

**Ease of Touring**

The three entrances require only a half step to enter the interior. The rose- and crème-colored marble floor is easily walked upon, considering its age.

Two steps are required to walk into the chapels. You need to climb two steps above the church's floor and walk to the side of the altar to see the Giulia Lama Altar painting.

**Bell Tower**

At the base of Santa Maria Formosa's Baroque bell tower, there is a grotesque mask built to "scare off the devil." The old bell and the even older grotesque mask complement each other. They represent the profane and the sacred existing together.

**Church Touring**

The **Greek cross** construction of the church contains fifty arches and thirty windows that maintain a light, airy atmosphere. Sixteen square columns support the many domes and apse ceiling of the eight chapels.

One of the few church altar paintings by a woman is found here. **The Virgin** with **St. Magnus** and **St. Peter** in **Venice, c.1710** by **Giulia Lama,** dominates a huge altarpiece by a woman who was a member of this parish. It is a painting of the Virgin tenderly presenting the Holy Child to St. Magnus Bishop and St. Peter. Venice, a splendidly dressed female symbol, is seen worshiping the saints on high. A painting of the patron of architects, **St. Barbara,** is also present. It was painted by **Palma il Vecchio** in 1509.

**The Last Supper** by **Leandro Bassano** is illuminated with vivid colors and good use of light in another part of the church. Other religious paintings cover three walls of this church, started in 639 and rebuilt after a number of fires and an earthquake in 1688. Mauro Codussi's remodeling in 1492 received the most credit for the uniqueness of the church's interior.

**Author's Comments:** This is a quiet, peaceful church to visit. The female presences, felt in this church, are unique. There are also restaurants nearby with good food, so you can sit, relax, and watch the gondolas continually moving through the canals near the back of the church.

## ✍ Giulia Lama, the Venetian Renaissance Woman

**Giulia Lama** was born in 1681 in the Venetian parish of **Santa Maria Formosa.** She was not only a very talented painter, but also a poet, mathematician, and inventor.

**Lama** was influenced by fellow painter **Giovanni Battista Piazzeltta** and trained by her father, **Agostino Lama.** She continued to use **Battista's** style of dramatic lighting and shading during her life. Her work **Judith and Holofernes** can be seen at the **Accademia Galleries** in Venice. Her painting of **Martyrdom of St. Eurosia** is found at the **Ca'Rezzonico Museum.** Her major contribution to church art is the altarpiece of **The Virgin Magnus and St. Peter in Venice** at **Chiesa Santa Maria Formosa.** Her artistic skills led to a career of painting and private and public figure work. **Lama** suffered the hostility that usually went along in the seventeenth century when women entered a field dominated by men. Writers failed to record many significant achievements, possibly because of this gender bias.

Giulia Lama moved in Venice's artistic circles from a very young age. At first she used strong contrasts of light. Later, she toned down these contrasts in line with the Venetian style of Tiepolo.

In a somewhat fictionalized film of her life, she was portrayed as having suffered Inquisition torture because of her romantic activities and knowledge of human bodies in some of her nude paintings.

**Giulia Lama** was reportedly gifted in mathematics, a skilled poet, and an inventor of the first machine that made lace. The lace-making machine was her idea to give women more time for their families and creativity.

**Lama** was capable of painting sensitive portraits such as **Young Man with a Turban,** as well as completing altarpieces like the one in her home church. She evidently lived to seventy-two years, but even her age is speculation since women did not achieve the same biographical prestige as men.

We can only wonder how much greater her creativity would have been in a more enlightened time.

# *Bovolo Palazzo*
## The Snail Spiral Staircase and a Unique Venetian Surprise

➢ **Interest**

If you were unable to make a trip to **Pisa**, take a trip to a Venetian "look-alike" tower that does not lean.

➢ **Vaporetto Dock: Rialto**

Boats: 1, 82, N

➢ **Address**

Corte del Bovolo 4299, San Marco, reachable by wheelchair

➢ **Admission: 3,00 euros**

➢ **Hours**

April–October 1000–1830, Daily

**Ease of Touring**

Turn right from the station and walk down the Grand Canal on Riva del Carbon. Turn left on Calle Cavalla, continue walking to **Campo Manin,** continue to Calle de la Vida, and then go left on Calle Locanda. A few steps on Calle Carte Contarini will lead you to the charming entrance to a courtyard with a big surprise! The surprise is a special circular staircase that takes you up to the top of the palace with a remarkable view.

This unusual staircase was built in 1499 to connect the floors of a Venetian trader's palace. He had visited Pisa and obviously liked the design of the tower. This sight can be reached from the Grand Canal by wheelchair with no blocking canal bridges.

Unfortunately, the Bovolo Palace is not wheelchair accessible. There is a stone bench on each landing. When you reach the top, the view of Venice is another unique photo opportunity.

It is suggested that you stop at **Campo Manin** on the way back to examine the statue of **Manin** and his pet **flying lion**. The symbol of Venice seems to be paying a special homage to one of the most important heroes of the canal city who helped it become a part of the country of Italy.

The entire trip to **Bovolo** will take you only a forty-minute walk if you go back to the vaporetto stop at Rialto.

**Author's Comments:** This tower provides a great photo opportunity of Venice. The Campo Manin has many interesting shops, restaurants, and usually some street entertainers to provide a pleasant stop.

# Ca'Rezzonico Dock—A Look into Palace Life

➢ **Vaporetto Dock: Ca' Rezzonico**
Boats: 1, N

➢ **Sights**
Ca' Rezzonico Museo
Carmini Church
Scuola Grande Carmini

➢ **Walk**
Campo Santa Margherita

Ca'Rezzonico museum ushers the visitor into a plush, 18th century, royal life of wealthy Venice.

A short walk from the rear of Ca' Rezzonico leads visitors down a picturesque canal to family and university life in the huge Santa Margherita Campo.

# Ca'Rezzonico Museum
## Eighteenth-Century Palace Life in Venice

➤ **Interest**

The city of Venice took over this palace to preserve and display the flamboyant lifestyle of the eighteenth century in Venice. You will be able to see beautiful art and the room decorations and furniture that were popular during this period. There is also an adjoining garden with statues, plaques, and a shallow pond filled with tortoises.

➤ **Vaporetto Dock: Ca Rezzonico**

Boat: 1

➤ **Directions**

After leaving the vaporetto dock, there is a small wooden bridge that takes you to the ground floor. A private dock is also available for water taxis to accommodate wheelchairs or seniors who have become weary of riding the vaporetto and want to arrive by gondola.

The second entrance to the museum for vaporetto-riding visitors who do not climb the bridge is from the back gate. Move to the first canal bridge by the Saint Barnabas Church over the small bridge and travel back to the rear of the museum and enter the back gate. There are only four short steps to reach the lift. The rear park also requires four steps to enter.

➤ **Address**
Ca'Rezzonico Museum
Dorsoduro, 3136

➤ **Admission**
Ground Floor Free / 8,00 euros for first and second floors

➤ **Hours**
April–October, Wednesday–Monday, 1000–1800
November–March, Wednesday–Monday, 1000–1700
Closed Tuesdays

## Easy Touring

The entrance is also the area for bathrooms, bookstore and the information office. There is a self-operating lift on this floor that will take you to the other floors of the museum. The floors are smooth and easy to travel, but there are some difficult elevation changes in the floor.

## Museum History

Like countless other large mansions in many countries, there was a history of families who, after building their homes, did not have the wealth to continue maintaining their luxuriousness.

There was an economic decline in Venice in the seventeenth century caused by Spain taking over much of the Eastern trade monopoly after Columbus' voyages to the new world. Many of Venice's wealthy families of this period fell on hard times.

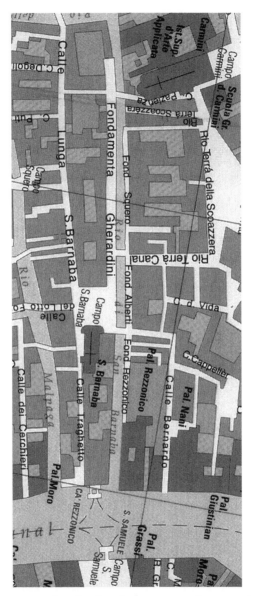

Canal San Barnaba leads the visitors from Ca'Rezzonico Museum past churches and vegetable boats to the Campo Santa Margherita.

**Robert Browning**, the English painter, and **John Singer Sargent**, the American painter, bought the building in 1889. Various people rented one floor or another, and several families took over the palace.

It was not until 1929 that the city of Venice began to think of restoring this former palace into an example of eighteenth-century life. Finally, in 1936, the city of Venice actually took over the palace and all its furnishings for the purpose of creating an art gallery that would best reflect this flamboyant time of Venice.

The present gallery reflects the wealth of this time by naming each of its rooms with its original palace function: **The Ballroom, The Nuptial Allegory Room, The Chapel, The Tapestry Room, The Throne Room,** and **The Tiepolo Room.**

At various times during the year special exhibits are on display. A large banner on the front of the palace facing the Grand Canal usually announces these exhibits.

**Ca'Rezzonico** ceiling frescoes makes one curious and somewhat uneasy with all the peering down from the multi-colored **gods** and **goddesses.**

### Museum Touring
**The ground floor** is basically the entrance to the museum from the Grand Canal and the land. It has a portico that takes one

from the Grand Canal to the coffee shop, bathrooms, ticket office, special exhibit room, and the garden in the rear.

**The first floor** has the radiant **Great Wall of Festivals** that held the many parties and balls of the rich seventeenth century. **The Nuptial Allegory Roma,** next to the outside minor canal, decorates the ceiling with the fresco **Merit Ascending** to the **Temple of Immortal Glory** by **Tiepolo,** with four impetuous white horses drawing Apollo's wagon bearing a wedding couple. **The Chapel,** the next room, was built by a future **pope** of the family, **Clement XIII Rezzonico**. It overlooks the outside canal, Rio di San Barnaba.

**The Pastel Room** contains the magnificent ceiling fresco, **The Triumph** of **Poetry** by Gaspare Diziani, with a chandelier and golden table.

**The Tapestry Room** is next with a golden tapestry, **Story of King Solomon and the Queen of Sheba** and a ceiling fresco, **Triumph of the Virtues** by **Jacopo Guiana**.

**The Throne Room** contains a **golden throne** and ceiling fresco, **Allegory of Merit** by **G. Tiepolo.**

**The first-floor passage** has a collection of porcelain and a painting, **Martyrdom of St. Eurosia** by **Giulia Lama,** the only recognized woman painter of seventeenth-century Venice.

**The Library** contains the remarkable marble **Veiled Woman** by **Antonio Corradini** with the ceiling fresco, **Allegorical Triumph** by **Mattia Bortoloni**.

**The Lazzarini Room** and **The Brustolon Room** contain fascinating furniture and a brutal **Jael and Sisera** by **Jacopo Amigoni**.

**The portico** on the **second floor** is reached by a staircase from the small gallery in the portico on floor one.

**The second floor** contains many worthwhile paintings. Visitors miss great works of art by not going to this floor. The **Punchinellos** of **G. Tiepolo** are in another room dedicated to **Tiepolo** and his special art.

**The third-floor Ai Do San Marchi' Chemist Shop** has been recreated to show a working chemist store that supplied medicine until 1908. It contains 183 decorated **Majolica** jars for spices and herbs, seventy-six decorated blue-patterned, white **Majolica** jars, and thirty-three jars in **Murano floor glass**. Also, a wonderful display of huge glass containers shows how the liquids are boiled and moved through glass tubes from one jar to another. This is a science exhibit of the sixteenth century.

**Author's Comments:** After you visit the many beautiful rooms in this museum, I suggest you return to the ground floor, walk straight to the back, and go outside to sit, rest, and see a lovely park. There are statues, plaques, a shallow pond filled with tortoises, and a small children's play yard. After resting, you may be ready to walk to the **Santa Margherita Campo**. The Santa Margarita Campo will also give you the opportunity to visit **Carmini Church**. On the way you will pass a greengrocer's barge moored in the canal.

## ᕬᕲ  The Mysterious Punchinellos by Tiepolo

**Ca'Rezzonico** ceiling frescoes makes one curious and somewhat uneasy with all the peering down from the multicolored **gods** and **goddesses,** but especially the **Punchinellos.** These hunchbacked, long-nosed characters in a special kind of white clothes and short "dunce" hats were seen in a lot of **Giandomenico Tiepolo's** frescoes and reliefs.

Three big wall scenes in **Ca'Rezzonico** show **Punchinello** and **The Acrobats, Punchinello** in **Love,** and **Punchinello's Departure**. There were many of these figures with masks of huge hooked noses. What was **Tiepolo** presenting in these artworks? **Filippo Pedrocco** writes, "He is a symbol of that part of humanity that still retains a primordial, spontaneous will to survive in the face of a society in rapid dissolution." These men in the white costumes represent the new "everyman" created by the **French Revolution**. Wisdom is no longer just possessed by royalty or the wealthy.

You can see many other **Punchinellos** in Ca'Rezzonico. They have also become very popular for **Carnevale,** appearing in almost every mask shop throughout Venice.

# The Walk to Santa Margherita Campo

> **Sights**
> Campo Barnaba
> Santa Maria dei Carmini
> Scuola Grande Dei Carmini
> Campo Santa Margherita

> **Vaporetto Dock: Ca Rezzonico**
> Boats: 1, 82

> **Interest**
> **Campo Santa Margherita** is the Dorsoduro main square. It is one of the liveliest in Venice and is the focal point for the whole community. By night, it is filled with students from the nearby university. The north part is dominated by the former church of Santa Margherita, now beautifully restored for use as a University of Venice Conference Hall.

This is one of the largest neighborhood centers, with restaurants, bars, and gelato shops second only to San Marco Square. You will find it filled day and night with Venetians shopping, gossiping, eating, drinking, dancing, and playing with their children.

Two beautiful sites anchor this campo, **Scuola Grande Dei Carmini** and **Santa Maria Carmini**, both well worth your time for viewing.

**Ease of Touring**

> **Campo San Barnaba:** Leave the vaporetto dock and walk on the left side of Rio Terra Canal through Campo S. Barnaba. Cross the bridge to the right on Rio Terra Canal.

> **Santa Maria dei Carmini:** Entrance to the church has only two steps; the floor of the interior is uncomplicated and easy to walk.

> **Scuola Grande Dei Carmini:** Entrance requires climbing four steps into a combined bookstore and ticket office. There is a public restroom behind the ticket office.

> **Campo Santa Margherita:** Leave the vaporetto and walk on the left side of Rio Terra Canal through Campo Barnaba. Cross the bridge to the right on Rio Terra Canal. Enter the campo on Calle de Pazienzea by Chiesa S.M. Carmini.

If you have visited the Ca Rezzonico Museum, leave through its rear door. Walk down the footpath on the right of Rio di Campo canal. Most days there are boat "stores" on the canal selling produce, antiques, and other products. These are usually moored near Campo Barnaba. Journey a short distance further, turn right at Rio Terra Canal, and walk to Campo Santa Margherita.

# Chiesa Santa Maria Carmini

This is possibly one of the most beautiful churches in Venice. It is filled with beautiful artwork, huge freestanding carved wood podiums, and lovely paintings up and down both sides of the center aisle. Along each side of the church are stations of religious paintings and statues.

American artist John Singer Sargent painted the beauty of this church many times. Carmelo Carmini was initially constructed in the sixteenth century, and B. Longhena completed much of it in the second half of the seventeenth century.

The interior is also decorated with these murals: **The Virgin in Glory, The Virtues,** and **The Angels** by G.B. Tiepolo between 1743 and 1744.

➢ **Church Touring**
The entrance to the church requires only two steps. The floor of the interior is uncomplicated and easy to walk. The side entrance by the canal is the easiest entry. The main entrance leads to the Santa Margherita Campo.

➢ **Directions**
The scuola is to the right of S.M. Carmini in another building

➢ **Location**
Santa Margherita Campo

➢ **Address**
Scuola Grande Dei Carmini
2617 Dorsoduro

➢ **Phone: 041.528.9420**

➢ **Hours**
900–1200 and 1500–1800 Daily except Sunday

### Scuola Touring
This Scuola Grande is in the process of becoming a hall for exhibits and concerts. This campo is also a popular place for Hollywood to film productions. You may recognize parts of it if you have seen the film *Casanova*.

### Campo Santa Margherita
The university students merge with Venetian family life in this square. You are encouraged to spend an afternoon just "hanging out." Or, just be there for the university-style nightlife that happens in Venice.

In the evening the pubs, restaurants, and coffeehouses come alive as excellent places of entertainment. If you have teenagers in your group, this is where they will want to be in the evening.

There is a thriving market set up on long tables covered by white canvas roofs, with music playing during the days.

You may choose to retrace your steps back by Campo Barnabas and its unique antique and produce boat stores. You might choose to walk by Ca' Rezzonico and relax in the coffee shop and garden and see if you would plan to return in a few days to see their display of royal life in the seventeenth century.

**Author's Comments:** Have fun exploring. Remember, you can't really get lost on these islands if you keep track of where the vaporetto boats journey to.

# *Accademia Dock—Gateway to Art*

➢ **Vaporetto Dock: Accademia**
Boats: 1, 82, N

➢ **Sights**
Gallerie Dell' Accademia
Peggy Guggenheim Collection
S.M. Della Salute

➢ **Concerts**
Chiesa S. Vidal

The Grand Canal with Regata boats, Salute domes, and the Guggenheim seen from the Accademia Bridge.

# *Accademia Gallery*
## The Gallery of the Venetian Academy

➤ **Interest**

Most significant cities in Italy had schools for art students. This gallery was Venice's art school. The 300 exhibits demonstrate the development of Venetian art. If you have a passion for famous religious painting, you will have only this opportunity to see them while you are in Venice.

➤ **Vaporetto Dock: Accademia**

Boats 1, 82, N

➤ **Location**

Dorsoduro, 1055 Venice

➤ **Phone: 041.522.2247**

➤ **Hours**

0815–1915 Daily except Sunday

➤ **Admission: 6,50 euros**

**Ease of Touring**

The entrance to the Accademia is only about twenty-five feet from the vaporetto dock at the southern end of the Accademia Bridge. The entryway to the gallery consists of three stone steps into a glass-door entrance. The lobby has a flat marble floor up to the ticket counter. The thirty steps up to the gallery make it a challenge for weak legs and impossible for wheelchairs. There is no elevator. Staff members have indicated that the building will be wheelchair accessible by 2011, including an elevator. The gallery will probably not be accessible until then. A large standard restroom is located just off exhibit room XII.

## Touring

**Napoleon** created this gallery from the artworks of the **Venetian Academy of Fine Arts** and two other galleries in 1800. These collections were crammed into several religious buildings that had been closed by his staff during his occupation of Venice.

The convent of **Lateran Canons Church of Carita'** and the **Scuola della Carita'** were combined into the present-day gallery.

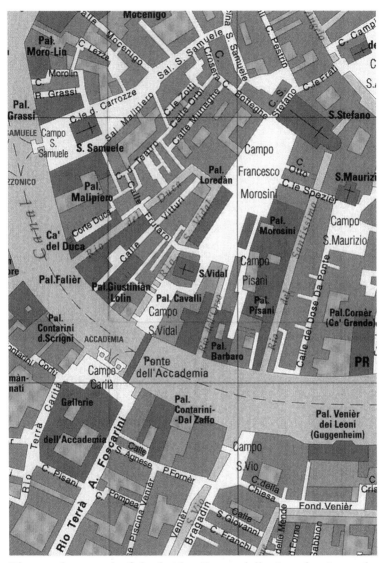

The southern end of the bridge Ponte della Accademia marks the location of the Accademia Gallery and vaporetto dock. The Guggenheim Collection and the SM Salute church can be reached by walking Calle S. Agnese to the east.

Rebuilding and restoration is proceeding to provide a protective surrounding for all the priceless religious, Renaissance, and modern paintings produced by Venice's artists.

These collections are placed in twenty-four exhibition rooms containing approximately 332 pieces of art. There are fifty-nine artists, including **Titian, Tintoretto, Bassano, Tiepolo,** and the famous Venetian female artist **Giulia Lama**.

### The Accademia Galleries

You are encouraged to follow the sequential number order of these rooms to get the effect of art progress in Venice from the twelfth to the nineteenth century.

The total gallery can be seen in about one and one-half hours if you just view each painting for a short visual journey. If you want more, rent the audio guide that describes each work of art. To really take home the experience, you are encouraged to buy *The Accademia Galleries in Venice* by **Giovanna Nepi Scire** from the bookstore.

## ᐈᐈ Gallery Room Contents by Subject or Artist

1   The Primitive
2   Great Fifteenth-Century Altarpieces
3   Bellini, Giorgione, Conegliano, Piombo and Diana
4, 5   Bellini, Mantegna, Francesca, Tura and Giorgione
6   Titian, Tintoretto and Veronese
7, 8   Lotto, Savoldo, Romanino and Palma il Vechio
10   Titian, Tintoretto and Veronese
11   Bassano, Strozzi, Tiepolo, Giordano, Tintoretto, Veronese & Pordenone
12   Ricci, Zais and Zuccarelli (RESTROOMS)
13   Bassano and Tintoretto
14   Seventeenth-Century Paintings
15   Pellegrini, Tiepolo and Guardi
16   Tiepolo and Ricci
16 A   Longhi, Piazzetta and Giulia Lama
17   Canaletto, Guardi, Tiepolo, Longhi and Carriera
18   Student works and Canova models
19   Montagna, Agostino da Lodi and Boccaccio
20   Miracle of the Relics of the Cross
21   Carpaccio's Legend of Saint Ursula
22   A Neoclassical Room
23   Former Church of Carita (Special Exhibits)
24   Former solo dell' Albergo of the Scuola di Santa Maria della Cartia.

*Eighty canvases of the work of artists can be viewed by special arrangement by calling: 041-522-2247*

**Author's Comments:** Remember, this is a work in progress. Venetians still resent how little space was originally made available by Napoleon's administration. The gallery is somewhat crowded with artwork.

# Guggenheim Collection
## The Peggy Guggenheim Collection of Modern Art

➤ **Interest**

This gallery was the private home of a remarkable American woman who became an important part of the art world in Venice. Marguerite "Peggy" saved a number of European artworks from possible Nazi destruction and helped pay for the escape of some Jewish artists.

➤ **Vaporetto Dock: Accademia**

Boats: 1, 82

➤ **Directions**

Take a few steps to the left from the Accademia dock to Rio Terra D. Carita. Walk to Calle S. Agnese and turn left. Cross the small bridge on Fondamenta Venier to the Guggenheim Gallery on the left.

➤ **Address**

Peggy Guggenheim Museum
Palazzo Venier dei Leoni
701 Dorsoduro, 30123 Venice

➤ **Phone: 041.240.5411**

Website: www.guggenheim.com

➤ **Admission: 10,00 Euros**

➤ **Hours**
Wednesday–Monday 1000–1800
Saturday 1000–2200
Closed Tuesday April–October

## Ease of Touring

This museum is not recommended for wheelchairs. It has stair challenges at several points in the buildings. This is a one-story home that was made into a gallery.

## Museum Touring

Peggy Guggenheim took her collection of modern art to New York during World War II and opened the Art of this Century Gallery. She moved to Venice after the war and opened her home as a museum in 1952. Her free-spirited life became a part of the Venetian art scene and resulted in this magnificent "Collezione" on the Grand Canal between the Accademia and the famous Chiesa Santa Maria Salute. Peggy Guggenheim lived her life as only she could live it until she died in 1979 at the age of 81. She willed her collection to the Guggenheim galleries of the world, and it continues to set the high standards for galleries in Venice today.

The gallery presents Peggy Guggenheim's personal collection of twentieth-century art, masterpieces from the Gianni Mattioli collection and the Nasher Sculpture Garden. All the major twentieth-century art movements are represented: abstract expressionism, surrealism, cubism, and constructivism. There are rooms full of Chagall, Klee, and Pollock. Masterpieces include Max Ernst's Robing of the Bride, Brancusi's Smooth Bird in Space, Victor Brauner's The Surrealist, Jackson Pollack's Circumcision, Picassso's The Poet, Joan Miro's Interno Olandese, and Henry Moore's Family Group. Alexander Calder's wonderfully moving mobiles are shown with Peggy's silver bedstead, made by him.

The staff continually augments this permanent collection with special exhibits of world-class European and American modern artists.

The buildings surrounding the terrace contain great art presented in a very effective manner. There is usually a special exhibitor whose work is accompanied by informative audio-visual presentations. You can enjoy the memorial patio garden gravesite of Peggy surrounded by her beloved dogs—fourteen in all—their names and dates of birth and death. Peggy also has the honor of being the last person in Venice to have her own private gondola and gondolier. Pictures may be taken of all exterior artworks.

When you move through both wings of the building and walk to the delightful Grand Canal Terrace with its statues, you will see one very interesting piece, a man on horse, nude, arms outstretched, and visibly aroused.

Sitting on the promontory over the canal provides a gorgeous 360-degree vista of both sides of the Grand Canal.

**Author's Comments:** Peggy Guggenheim's life is well documented in *Mistress of Modernism,* by Mary V. Dearborn. The gallery makes a pleasant visit to see art and a beautiful place to view the Grand Canal.

# Basilica di Santa Maria Della Salute

> **Interest**
>
> This landmark basilica was built as an offering to the Virgin Mary for ending the plague of 1784 in Venice.

> **Vaporetto Dock: Salute**
>
> Boat: 1, 82

> **Directions**
>
> Take a short vaporetto ride to the Salute Dock. If you want an interesting stroll to Basilica Salute from Accademia Dock, walk to the left side of the gallery and move down Rio Terra A. Foscarini to Calle S. Agnese. Cross the small canal bridge on Fondamenta Venier to the Guggenheim Gallery on the left, continue across three small canal bridges to the basilica.

> **Admission: Free**

> **Hours**
>
> Daily 900–1200, 1500–1730

> **Phone: 042.522.5558**

**Ease of Touring**

The vaporetto stops in front of the basilica entrance. I recommend the use of the handrails provided on the right side of the sixteen stone steps. The smooth floor is a beautiful red, white, and yellow marble; this is an easy cathedral to visit.

## Basilica Touring

This unique building was constructed to replicate a crown for the **Virgin Mary**. This freestanding domed cathedral is a common visual landmark for Venice. It has six chapels around its unusual circular interior. There is a small altar area on one side. A design converges on a central circle of five roses suggesting the decades, or five clusters of ten beads, of the Rosary. A grouping of statues dramatically demonstrate the Virgin Mary's actions in saving Venice.

A plague had killed about one-third of its citizens. This led the Venetian Senate to vow, to the Virgin Mary, to build a church if the deaths would stop. Reportedly, the deaths stopped and the Senate agreed to build this remarkable octagonal basilica. The basilica and its dramatic steps of white Istrian stone are built on 1.2 million wooden pilings that remain intact after more than 300 years.

Each year on November 21, Salute is the location of a remarkable festival that involves building a pontoon bridge that spans the Grand Canal. Celebrants cross this bridge to worship at Salute and the Virgin Mary. Venetians walk across this bridge over the water from San Marco to the basilica to receive the Virgin's blessing. The gondoliers even bring their oars for a priest to bless at this holy celebration.

A painting by **Tintoretto**, the **Wedding at Cana,** can be seen when the sacristy is open. The critic **Ruskin** pointed out it was almost impossible to spot the bride and groom in this painting.

Visitors are encouraged to examine the building at the tip of the peninsula to the right. It is the **Dogana di Mare** and was extremely important to Venetians in their trade with the outside world.

**Author's Comments**: This landmark is worth visiting for many reasons. The view of Venice across the Grand Canal is a major one. On most sunny days, you will find artists set up with their easels, painting the fine view of Venice that is available. Wonderful pictures can be taken of the canal, lagoon, and the passing boats.

# San Toma Dock—Treasures of Religion and Art

➤ **Vaporetto Dock: San Toma**
Boats 1, 82, N

➤ **Sights**
Basilica di Santa Maria Gloriosa dei Frari
Scuola Grande di San Rocco
Chiesa San Rocco

➤ **Concerts**
Basilica Dei Frari

This minor canal leads to one of most important artistic/ religious centers of Frari Basilica, Chiesa San Rocco, and Scuola Grande Rocco.

An immense collection of centuries of religious art and memorials to Venice's great artists is found in the Frari Basilica.

# Basilica of Santa Maria Gloriosa Dei Frari

> ## Interest

This particular site starts a basic training in Venetian religious art from the twelfth century. Scuola Grande Rocco and Chiesa de Rocco are located just around the corner, and they join Frari as one of the spiritual artistic centers of Venice.

> ## Vaporetto Dock: San Toma

Boat: 1, 82, N

> ## Directions

There are a number of signs on buildings from the vaporetto stop that read "Chiesa Dei Frari" and "Scuola Grande Rocco." If you follow these signs, you will get to the Frari easily. Look particularly for Scuola Grande or Frari. Most of these passages are only wide enough to allow two or three people to walk side by side. You will see the red bricks of the Frari building after going about ten minutes from the dock.

> ## Address

Campo dei Frari
Basilica dei Frari
S.Polo 3072

➢ **Admission: 2,50 euros**

➢ **Hours**
900–1800, Monday–Saturday / 1300–1800, Sunday

➢ **Phone: 041.272.8611**

**Ease of Touring**

Visitors are encouraged to enter through the nearest side entrance of Frari for ease of entry. This ground-floor entrance leads into an almost completely unobstructed marble floor.

The coffee bar and restaurants across the bridge have restrooms. Buy a drink and you are welcome to use the facility.

There are no handrails to climb the short flights of marble steps to the altars and the interiors of the chapels.

Most of the sienna and crème-colored floors and steps are worn from centuries of use. Be careful. Some of the tombstones on these floors are a little wobbly when you walk on them. The floor is blocked at the wooden choir by three steps. Evening concerts provide an entry on the left side to the front of the cathedral that avoids these steps but does require stepping down four steps.

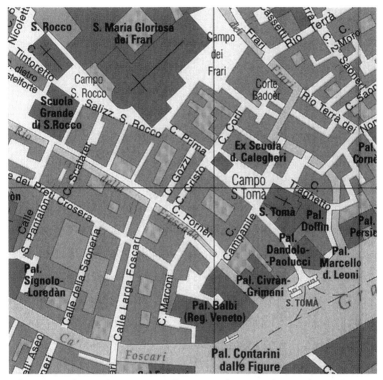

This map shows how to reach Frari, the Scuola, and San Rocco from S. Toma Dock.

## Basilica's History

The early Realtino (Rialto) Republic centered at the only bridged part of the Venetian islands. These people welcomed the followers of Francis of Assisi a little after 1200 CE. The doge saw the constant physical labor of the brothers as a good example for citizens. The Franciscan order earned a reputation as builders and helpers of the poor.

Doge Jacopo Tiepolo gave the "lesser" friars a plot of land in the district of San Stefano called San Stin. They built a monastery and a small church in 1231. Several larger churches were needed with the increased size of the congregation and brotherhood. A larger monastery was also built.

By 1582 five altars with priceless works of art by Donatello, Vivarini and Titian, and a precious wooden choir with stalls carved by Marco Cozzi were present. This choir screen is a mixture of Gothic work by Bartolomeo Bon and Renaissance elements by the Lombardo family. The absolute masterpiece was the high altarpiece: **The Assumption** by **Titian.**

Napoleon closed down the Franciscan order in Venice in 1809 and used the buildings for a storehouse. The Venetian annexation by the Kingdom of Italy led to a return of the Franciscans. The continuing growth of the present edifices demonstrates the Franciscan return to Venice in all its glory.

## The Interior

The basilica's internal structure developed into a Latin cross with a transept, a nave, and two aisles separated by twelve mighty pillars. Wooden tie beams, a central apse, and three minor apse chapels on each side link the tops of these pillars. The ceiling has a Gothic cross vaulting at the midpoint of this huge hall.

## Basilica Touring

Some feel uneasy when they enter Frari. Some say it's just a "big gloomy barn." Others have been concerned about the variety of "artwork" plastered around in a kind of haphazard fashion. Some are even concerned about the politically incorrect statues over one of the entry doors. These critics forget that this was a living, breathing church center for over eight centuries. The marvelous wood carvings, marble statues, huge memorials, and accumulated frescoes and oil paints can't just be set aside in a museum or thrown away.

It is a collection of spontaneous spiritual artwork and the labor of thousands of men and women who followed the leadership of St. Francis of Assisi and St. Clare of Assisi to build places of worship and help the needy. If you visit Santa Croce Basilica in Florence, Italy, you will see the same joyous accumulation of artwork from the twelfth century to the nineteenth century.

The outside of Frari is the usual Franciscan plan for simplicity. It is embellished with ogival portals in the red stone of Verona and Byzantine pillars in white Istrian stone. Antique bas-relief frames the portals. The façade is in a late Gothic style. The front entrance has a bas-relief depicting Mary with the Christ child and angels. Above the entrance arch is a statue of the **Risen Christ** by **Alessandro Vitoria,** 1581.

Once you have purchased your ticket at the entrance, turn and look at all the art that you have just walked under. Some visitors miss it completely! The entrance is covered with monuments and paintings by Floriani and Muttoni and is called the counter-façade.

## Monument Row

The most striking monument is the **Canova Pyramid**. It turns out that the sculptor Canova designed it for the artist Titian. When that remarkable painter died from the plague, the memorial was forgotten. Then, when Canova died, his many admirers decided that it would be most appropriate as his memorial.

Titian was forgotten until 300 years after his death. Austrian rulers decided it was time to bury this fine creator of world-famous altars and paintings, such as **The Assumption.** They brought Titian's remains from the Plague Burial Island, and he was buried in the large memorial across from the Canova Pyramid.

### The Choir Directors' Dream

Anyone who has sung in a choir will appreciate the central jewel of the building. You can marvel at the work of Marco Cozzi, who, in 1468, created a place for choir members' voices to be amplified by the woodwork. This choir musical platform enabled voices to compete with the sound of the two organs in this majestic setting.

The chapel to the left of the choir contains the only **Donatello** work in Venice, the wooden statue of St. John the Baptist. Visitors are sometimes shocked at the ugly appearance of this portrayal of John as they are Donatello's Mary Magdalene currently housed in Florence's Duomo Opera Museum. Each demonstrates the tremendous suffering of these two souls in their lifetime projected by the artist.

The centerpiece, however, is the **Assumption** by **Titian**. This altar was consecrated in 1469. **Mary** seems to be aware that she will have a child. Members of the order described how they were waiting for a miracle. Indeed, they found one. The painting complemented and brought to life all of the surrounding works of art.

A sacred crucifix made in 1200 portrays **Christ** hanging on a cross. It is to the left of the **Assumption** painting. This Christ was repainted by unknown artists during the period of the closure of **Frari** by **Napoleon.**

The present splendid crucifix uncovered under the eleventh-century painting, represents the complete death of **Christ**. Others see it as acceptance of **Christ**'s humanity.

**Author's Comment:** Now that you've received your basic training in "church art," walk to the rear of the basilica and move about a hundred steps to the right to the **Scuola Grande di San Rocco** for your "graduate course" by the artist **Tintoretto.**

# Scuola Grande di San Rocco
## School of St. Roch

➢ **Interest**

Venice is "Tintoretto Territory." While in Venice, you can experience a massive amount of this great artist's work in this building.

➢ **Vaporetto Dock: S. Toma**

Boats: 1, 82, N

➢ **Directions**

Follow a series of signs that read "Scuola Grande di San Rocco" and "Basilica Dei Frari" from the vaporetto dock. These signs will lead you along passages through small campos that are clearly marked. You will know when you reach your destination when you see the church of Saint Roch and the Scuola Grande on your left.

➢ **Address**

Campo San Rocco
San Polo, 3054

➢ **Admission: 5,50 euros**

➢ **Hours**

0800–1200, 1400–1600 Daily

## Ease of Touring

Visitors can see the four major rooms of the Scuola only after climbing five marble steps at the entrance of the building. This semicircular staircase has no handrails. Wheelchair riders can enter on a flat floor through a door to the right of the main entrance.

The first room, the **Ground Floor Hall,** doubles as a concert hall and a gallery for eight huge **Tintoretto** paintings. The main exhibition hall of thirty-eight paintings is at the top of two spectacular flights of marble stairs with thirty-three steps.

A stair-climbing machine resembling a wheelchair with rubber tank-like tracks works with assistance in climbing the stairs. The ticket seller should be contacted for its use. There is no public restroom in this building.

## Touring

**Scuola Grande di San Rocco** is a huge treasure of art and humanity's effort to care for kindred human beings. One person, the artist **Tintoretto**, filled it with his own contributions of sixty religious paintings. The charitable goodwill of thousands of Venetians in their Scuolas worked to help people qualify for jobs in Venice's growing economy in the fourteenth through seventeenth centuries. Prisoners' families were given food and shelter to survive in this city of canals. This was one of many semi-religious organizations to provide charity to the less fortunate.

This organization gathered many expensive-looking possessions over the hundreds of years it existed. It is tempting to question its richness; however, one can focus on the magnificence of its purpose and the beauty of its contents.

There are four major rooms to view: **The Ground Floor Hall** that you enter at the ticket office holds concerts and presentations given to the public. This is the last room to be decorated by the major artist **Tintoretto** and represents his most controversial artwork of religious philosophy.

**The Great Upper Hall** must be reached by climbing a magnificent marble staircase. It contains many woodcarvings and oil paintings. It has an appearance of a huge church auditorium covered with rich decor and twenty-five paintings by **Tintoretto** all over the ceiling and walls. It is here, surrounded by religious art, that the membership met to plan charitable works.

This was the second room to be decorated. Make sure you have your best glasses with you. In fact, if you have a pair of field glasses or binoculars, bring them along to look at the paintings on the ceiling and walls. There are plenty of chairs, so sit down and look at the total room.

It would be wise to rent an audio guide when you begin a search of the walls. Carved wood figures cover the walls. In fact, the first one at the front side is a portrait of **Tintoretto** in his later years. Notice that there are a number of vocations and careers represented by these carved figures.

### The Albergo Hall

This important hall can be reached off of **the Great Hall** and was the first to be decorated. Huge paintings of the life of **Christ** and many ceiling paintings, including one about **Saint Rocco,** can take one's breath away. This is not the only scuola in Venice, but it is the favorite of many visitors.

**Author's Comments:** Look for the fast brush strokes that **Tintoretto** used that almost drove his competitors crazy. This was the big controversy among his peers—he worked too fast!

## ᕬᕤ Tintoretto Jacopo Robusti–The Nature of Tintoretto

**Tintoretto** demonstrated that he was very self-confident as an artist and as a Christian. He also was not your "puppet-on-a-string" artist who would do anything to sell his work.

When the committee of the **Scuola Grande di Rocco** advertised their intention to have **The Albergo Room** decorated, they requested "cartoons" or paper sketches from artists who wished to apply for the job. Many artists submitted sketches, but not **Tintoretto.** He submitted a completed painting! His painting of **Saint Rocco** was accepted by the committee because of its strength and his speed. His headstrong action paid off. He got that commission and many more.

A recent cleaning of his paintings revealed through special laboratory techniques that he always started his paintings by sketching directly on the canvas, not paper. Also, they found that he sketched figures in the nude, to make sure they were anatomically correct. Then he would cover them with clothing when he was completing the painting.

In spite of this care, his paintings were completed so fast that he earned the nickname of Tintoretto Dyer, or someone who produces colors by soaking material in a pot. He could complete three pictures in the time it took the artists of that period to paint one. His "brushes are too big," "his strokes are too fast," and "his paintings lack detail" were the cries of his fellow artists.

Why would he need extreme detail with a painting that was going to be on the ceiling of the **Upper Hall**?

When you are in the great hall of **Scuola Rocco,** look at his ceiling paintings with the mirrors they provide, to see the work better. Can you detect any missing details? Probably not. **Tintoretto** liked to paint and did it well. His contemporaries objected to his speed and the church disliked the license he took in his religious art presentations.

Two paintings on the **Ground Floor Hall** demonstrated his controversial religious themes. Look at **St. Mary Magdalen** and **St. Mary in Egypt.** He portrays Mary Magdalene as someone who finds magic in nature. The places she is shown have an iridescent look to them, and she appears quite happy to be alone. **Dan Brown's** *The Da Vinci Code* presents her as someone special who had a possible romantic relationship with **Christ.** Perhaps **Tintoretto** felt these same possibilities when he painted her in this picture. His speed is documented by the number of paintings he produced decorating these three rooms of **Scuola Grande di Rocco**.

| | | |
|---|---|---|
| **Albergo Hall** | **1564–1567** | **twenty-seven paintings** |
| **Upper Hall** | **1576–1581** | **twenty-five paintings** |
| **Ground Floor Hall** | **1582–1587** | **eight paintings** |

Art history specialists add another problem that faced him. Three colors he used in his paintings darkened after some years. Imagine how bright and colorful his paintings would be if some of his paint pigments had not failed him. The following pigments changed: blue to lead grey, green to brown, and red to pink.

Religious historians point out that his later paintings shown in the **Ground Floor Hall** depicted Christianity in a more modern mode. This man improved as a painter and changed as a Christian. All the while he painted for virtually just the costs of the paints, canvases, and frames.

This prolific painter and his family painted in a number of churches and the **Doge's Palace. Scuola Grande di San Rocco** gives one a chance to see the development of this man's skills as a painter and philosopher.

# *Chiesa San Rocco*
## Church of Saint Roch

➢ **Interest**

A ceremonial doge and the citizens of Venice make annual pilgrimages to this saint.

➢ **Vaporetto Dock: S. Toma**

Boat: 1, 82, N

➢ **Directions**

Follow a series of signs that read **"Scuola Grande di San Rocco"** and **"Basilica Dei Frari"** from the vaporetto dock. These signs will lead you along passages through small campos that are clearly marked and easy to follow. You will know when you reach your destination when you see the church of **Saint Roch** and the **Scuola Grande** on your left.

➢ **Admission: 5,50 euros**

➢ **Hours**

Daily 800–1230, 1400–1600

**Ease of Touring**

The interior of this church is flat and uncomplicated. It can be entered after climbing seven marble stairs, without the aid of handrails.

**Church Treasures**

The bones of **Saint Roch** are located behind the altar in a specially built religious display. The church is dedicated to him and his life is described by nineteen paintings by **Tintoretto, Giuseppe Angeli, Sabastiano Ricci, Pordenone, G. Fumiani, F. Solimenta,** and **A. Schiavone**.

**Rocco** studied medicine as a youth. As the plague swept Europe, decimating the population of major cities, he decided to leave his wealthy family. He gave up his riches and devoted himself to healing the victims of the plague.

These deeds of goodness immediately earned him veneration in France. He was called upon as a protector against the pestilence, which was still raging through Europe. When he returned to his family's home, they would not recognize him. He died poor and in jail in 1327 at the age of thirty-two.

His following was particularly important in Venice, where his body was brought in 1485 and laid to rest in the church of the **Arch brotherhood** in 1520. It is thought that the delay in his burial was from the Venetian practice of burying victims of the plague in a special plague island.

After the great plague in 1576, he was proclaimed co-patron of the city and his church became a place of pilgrimage every year for the doge and the crowds of believers.

Even today, his date of return in August is celebrated solemnly, and a canopy called "Tendon del Doge" (the doge's canopy) is erected in St. Roch Square between the church and the scuola.

## Dog Lovers' Attention

You will be interested in how Roch survived during a siege of the plague by himself in the forest. According to Roch, an unknown dog brought bread to him during the time he was confined to a cave in the forest. He felt it was help from God. A large painting attesting to this story is on display at the **Accademia Museum.**

**Author's Comments:** Many visitors miss this little church when they visit **Scuola Grande di San Rocco** and **Basilica Frari.** It is small, intimate, and very restful with wonderful paintings to view.

# *Giglio Dock*
## An Unusual Church and a World-Class Opera House Partially Under Water

➢ **Vaporetto Dock: S. Giglio**
Boat: 1

➢ **Sights**
SM Del Giglio and La Fenice Opera House

➢ **Concerts**
La Fenice Opera House

SM Giglio seems to be a church dedicated to rectifying the bad reputation of a disgraced admiral of the Venetian Navy. The façade is covered with "angels" strangely similar to members of his family.

This newly reconstructed La Fenice opera house shows Venice at its supreme elegance. One can almost see Casanova flitting from one female inhabited box to another.

# Chiesa Giglio

> **Interest**
> This church was built by an admiral who was dismissed for incompetence during a war with **Crete**. It appears he has tried to cover this shame with a glorious church dedicated to himself.

> **Vaporetto Dock: S. Giglio**
> Boat: 1

> **Directions**
> Walk directly down Calle Rio di S. Maria Giglio from the vaporetto stop. This narrow walk opens up onto the Campo and the church site.

> **Location**
> Campo Santa Maria Giglio

> **Phone: 041.275.0462**

> **Admission: 3,00 euros**

> **Hours**
> 1000–1700 Monday–Sunday

**Ease of Touring**

Entrance of the church requires three stone steps. After the entrance, the floor is flat, smooth marble. Two treasury rooms can be viewed by window from the regular floor or require one step down for the viewer to be nearer the exhibit.

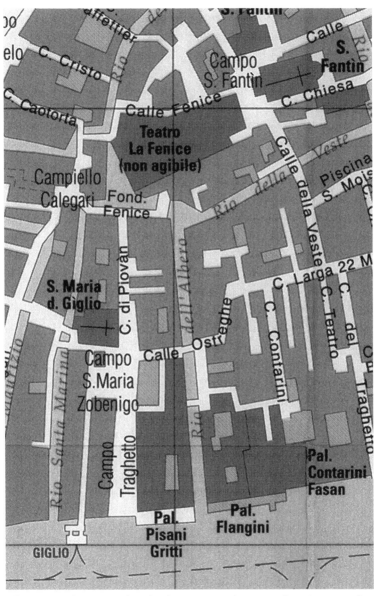

The route from Giglio dock to La Fenice can be seen on this map.

## Church Touring

The church is an appropriate pause for those scurrying on their way from the vaporetto stop to the **La Fenice Opera House.**

The interior of the church has a white marble façade and a high arched ceiling with several paintings on it. A number of ornate white marble decorations appear along the walls behind the altar.

A striking, unfinished-looking statue of a human on his or her knees in supplication, with head raised facing toward heaven, is on the floor before the lectern of the minister. Light filtering from the ceiling and gives this statue a marvelous, unreal look. The sacristy is located off to the right of the entrance. It has many church relics, altarpieces, and icons to view. No effort is made to stop flash photographs.

Outside, each of the four members of the disgraced admiral's family has a life-sized statue at eye level on the façade. The upper center of the façade has a large figure, which, at first glance, could be **Christ,** but on closer inspection it appears to be the admiral. Across the bottom are five relief sculptures of the forts and sea battles that this wealthy man seems to have won.

## 〰 **Decadence or Art?**

This church is really a huge exercise in defiant self-glorification by **Admiral Antonio Barbaro,** who was dismissed by the **doge** for incompetence during the **War of Crete**. The paintings inside are mostly by **Antonio Zanchi**. One such painting is **Ulysses Recognized by His Dog**, another piece of **Barbaro** self-mythologizing.

The church's front is like a big picture storybook, which was yet another façade that drew the censure of **John Ruskin**, author of **The Stones of Venice.** Ruskin could not get over the total lack of any **Christian** symbols (give or take a token angel or two).

**Mr. Ruskin's** critical mission of Venetian architecture was to discredit "the pestilent art of the **Renaissance**" in favor of the "healthy and beautiful" **Gothic** and its softer, Oriental Venetian variant.

**Mr. Ruskin** seems to have chosen the critical mission of deciding what is good and bad architecture in Venice. You will see the fusion of **Roman Byzantine Gothic** and **Arabic** features evident from just about any point of view on the Grand Canal.

**Author's Comment:** The church is a worthwhile pause as you scurry on your way to the La Fenice Opera House. There is an interesting shop in the campo of brocade fabric, tassels, pillows, and sometimes a sleeping cat. You may also be gifted with operatic arias from opera-hopeful street singers.

# La Fenice Opera House

➤ **Interest**

It took 18,000 to 20,000 canal boatloads of materials to rebuild this opera house after it was destroyed by fire in 1996. It is now a world-class concert and opera house. Even though you may not be an opera lover, the beauty and the engineering feat of rebuilding this work of art should not be overlooked.

➤ **Vaporetto Dock: Giglio**

Boat: 1

➤ **Location**

Calle della Fenice

➤ **Phone: 041-984-252**

➤ **Tickets**

Vivaldi Box Office, 20,00–100,00 euros, depending on seat location and production

➤ **Tours**

Available all year. Call for date, time, and language preferred.

**Ease of Touring**

La Fenice is wheelchair accessible. Walk from the dock down a long narrow passageway (Calle Gritti o del Campanile) to the Santa Maria Giglio Church. Pass in front of the church on campo Maria Zobenigo; the street dead-ends at a canal. Take the walkways to the left around a building to the front of La Fenice.

## Rebuilding the Legend

La Fenice was originally built for an audience of approximately 900. Some progressive citizens wanted to expand it to accommodate 1,200. The people of Venice almost revolted over whether the burned-out hulk should be recreated or expanded to a larger capacity. The romantics of the city won out with the original capacity of 900. You will see a modern fire-safe structure concealed by the elegance of soft muted colors. You will also see stairways, a lift, and wheelchair movers built in the necessary places. The restoration story is quite amazing.

The largest opera house in Venice is aptly called La Fenice (The Phoenix). It has burned several times. During the last fire, on the evening of January 29, 1996, the people of Venice were weeping in the streets. They watched their pride and joy burn completely to its foundation.

The loss was a catastrophe for Venetians. Verdi had premiered five of his operas in this house. The fact that arson may have been involved made the loss even more bitter. This catastrophe inspired author John Berendt to fly to Venice and write the book *The City of Falling Angels*. Mr. Berendt used his investigative journalist skills to reveal the truth about this fire.

Public reaction led to a mayor being jailed because of his incompetence. There was an eight-year battle, limited competency, planning, and concerns of whether it should be rebuilt as it was or replaced by a higher-capacity building.

The construction was a miracle of logistics when one considers that everything that's used in Venice must come in on a boat from eighteen to thirty feet long and no more than seven or eight feet wide. Every steel beam, piece of stone, and length of flooring had to fit into one of these boats. Part of the area under the building is underwater and encapsulated in watertight cement.

The many miracles preformed in this construction result in a picture-perfect opera house with appropriate space, safety, and acoustics. The author witnessed the rebuilt beautiful auditorium in October 2004, with its replaced rococo appearances of angels, vixens, and chandeliers. Pale mint green colors and soft plush, ornate chairs surround the visitor. Just sitting in this beautiful opera house gives one an uplift that music can only enhance.

Walking through the ornate front doors and up the white marble steps, you are dazzled by multiple huge crystal chandeliers lighting the entire entrance.

Ushers are ready to take you to your seats in this remarkable building. You expect to see Don Juan, Casanova, and many of the famous Venetian courtesans of the seventeenth century looking out of the elegant theater boxes. There are four levels of these boxes with up to thirty-five intimate elegant rooms on each level. There is space for four to eight individuals in each box. Your box will have not only seating, but also a gold-trimmed mirror and an elegant gold coat tree. There are exquisitely appointed lights on each side of the boxes, adding to the glamour and beauty of this building.

A "Standing Room Only" row is at the ceiling level. The balance of the audience is seated on the slightly elevated orchestra floor. The first ten rows from the stage are removed to make room for a larger orchestra.

Your companion, who may become a bit bored, need never be so rude as to look at a watch. He or she can just glance at the ceiling near the stage and read the time on a huge beautiful clock.

Attendance is like being inside a lavishly decorated candy box, with color filigree, paintings of angels, cherubs, and all the elegance that Venice could muster in its wealthy past.

The curtain glides open like huge velvet arms exposing the stage as a romantic interlude, inviting you to become a part of the performance.

The orchestra seats are similar to pale pink lounge chairs matching the color of all the other chairs in the building. Acoustics are remarkable when you hear singers singing without microphones.

For your first time attending the beautiful theater, you may want to arrive at a canal side entrance by gondola and relive the luxury of eighteenth-century Venice.

If you see no other sights in Venice, you have to put La Fenice at the must-see level. This alone can make your trip a truly wonderful experience to relive long after you have returned home.

**Author's Comment**: Being inside this opera house is like stepping back in time to an age of elegant beauty and gorgeous opulence. It is a wonderful place not only to hear but also to feel the beauty of the music. This wonderful experience will stay in your memory forever.

# *San Stae Dock*
## Art and Walk to a Rare Jewel of Venice

➢ **Vaporetto Dock: S. Stae**
Boats 1, N

➢ **Sights**
International Gallery of Modern Art
Campo Della Orio Walk
Chiesa S. Giacomo Dell' Orio

A pleasant walk from S. Stae Church takes visitors to a
remarkable campo of Venetian family life. This walk presents a
glimpse of apartment life seldom seen in Venice.

# Ca' Pesaro
## International Gallery of Modern Art

> ### Interest
> This is one of the largest palaces on the Grand Canal. Huge, magnificent paintings by well known artists are on view. Most visitors express joy and surprise at the impact of this gallery.

> ### Vaporetto Dock: St. Stae
> Boats 1, N

> ### Directions
> Leave the vaporetto dock in front of the church of the same name, **St. Stae. Ca' Pesaro's** amazing white building with a large stone façade of pointed blocks can be seen from the Grand Canal. However, to get to its entrance requires walking up a fourteen-step metal bridge to the left. Go to the right for a few steps and turn left on Pesaro behind the building. Continue on to the gallery entrance. An alternative route is available for those challenged by this steel bridge. Start at the right side of St. Stae Church and move down Salizzada di S. Stae to the second street called S. de Magazen. Cross the less challenging canal bridge, turn left and go onto Rimpetto, continue on Mocenigo, turning right on Pesaro, and go to the gate of Ca' Pesaro.

If you wish, walk to **Rialto Bridge.** You can do that by leaving the museum on the opposite side that you entered and following the signs to **Rialto.**

➢ **Address**
International Gallery of Modern Art
Santa Croce 2070
Fondamenta Pesaro Venice 30125

➢ **Phone: 041.524.0695 / Fax: 041.524.1075**

➢ **Admission: 5,50 euros, free for children under twelve**

➢ **Hours**
Winter 1000–1700, Summer 1000–1800

**Easy Touring**

Enter the gallery by walking down three marble steps through the glass door at the rear of the building. This is one of the few galleries that will provide wheelchairs for visitors by request. The many helpful attendants are easily identified by their uniforms; feel free to consult the staff for assistance. This building also has very convenient self-operating elevators to all of the floors.

A section on Oriental art is displayed on the second floor. It is not as accessible to wheelchairs as are the other floors of the gallery. The second floor will undergo change and may already have been transformed to a temporary exhibition floor with improved accessibility. Restrooms are available in the area before you enter the ground floor entrance.

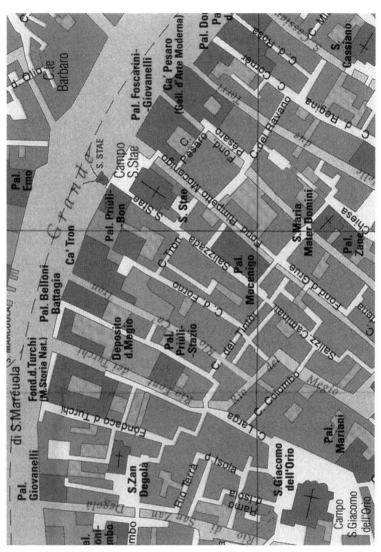

This map shows how you can walk to Ca' Pesaro, Orio or Rialto from the S. Stae Vaporetto dock.

**Gallery Touring**

**The Ca' Pesaro Palace** has an interesting exterior of Istrian stone and is one of the broadest and most monumental edifices on the entire Grand Canal. It's actually three buildings combined into one huge palace. Two architects, **Baldassare Longhena** and **Antonio Gaspari**, completed the palace work decades apart, and it reflects some inconsistencies. It is one of the marvelous examples of civil architecture and one of the most original palaces in the city.

Three floors of incredible paintings and sculpture are displayed in large easy-to-view rooms. Paintings that have rarely been exhibited because of their exceptional size are on display.

**Ground Floor**

The spaciousness of the entrance hall off the Grand Canal contains sculpture pieces of twentieth-century Italian art. **Adolfo Wildt's The Pure Madman, Francesco Messina's Eve,** and **Giacomo Manzu's The Cardinal** are outstanding examples.

**First Floor**

The first floor is the permanent collection area with nine large gallery rooms plus the Central Hall. (Some art may be out on loan to other countries or galleries. One must consider this possibility when visiting any significant world gallery like Ca' Pesaro.) The following rooms contain almost 200 pieces of nineteenth- and twentieth-century canvases and sculptures.

| | |
|---|---|
| Room I | Nineteenth-Century Venetian |
| Room II | Nineteenth-Century Italian |
| Central Hall | Biennale |
| Room III | Adolfo Weldt Collection |
| Room IV | Morandi to Kandinsky |
| Rooms V and VI | The Ca' Pesaro Movements |
| Room VII | Post War Art |
| Room VIII | 1950s Italian |
| Room IX | Venice—New Front and Spatialism |

**The Laugh,** by Russian **Philip Maljavine**, depects a wonderful group of peasants caught in a moment of joy. I am sure it will bring a smile and give you a feeling of participation. **Sewing the Sail,** by **Joaquin Sorolla y Bastida,** shows the terrace of a fisherman's house. It is joyfully enlivened by the work around an immense, very bright sail. The summer's day seems to materialize in the whiteness of the sail. Lastly, **John Lavery's Woman in Pink** displays a tragic expression on a beautiful woman's face. It may cause you to wonder about her life and circumstance.

The famous **Judith II/Salome** by **Gustav Klimt** is displayed in all of its glory, and a very interesting piece by **Marc Chagall,**

**The Rabbi of Vitebsk,** is an extraordinary figure of a Jew, not necessarily a rabbi, in the specific costume for Morning Prayer on non-festive days. The kippah on his head, the white tallith with black stripes on his shoulders, and tefillin on his forehead and left arm are outstanding. These are just a few of the wonderful pieces to be seen in this truly amazing International Gallery of Modern Art.

Some of the other artists whose works are exhibited:

- Raul Dufy
- Max Ernst
- Paul Klee
- Max Lieberman
- Henri Matisse
- Henry Moore
- Joan Miro
- Auguste Rodin
- Yves Tanguy

**The second floor** has a very complete Oriental art collection. This, however, is in a smaller area and not quite as easily accessible as the other two floors of work.

**Author's Comments:** This is a fascinating gallery with huge rooms that can display paintings that you can see very few places. It is truly one of the crown jewels of the Grand Canal.

# Chiesa San Stae, the Walk to Campo San Giacomo dell' Orio Campo and Church
## Rare Jewel of Italian Life Style

➢ **Interest**

Take a break from the tourist sights, stroll down an Italian shopping street, and then go out into a beautiful campo where you can relax with wine, coffee, and good food. Enjoy the Italian experience. There is a beautiful twelfth-century church, with a roof built by boat builders. You should try to visit this active family church while you are in Venice.

➢ **Vaporetto Dock: S. Stae**

Boats: 1, N

➢ **Directions**

Leaving the dock, walk straight down Salizada S. Stae, which turns right on Calle Dell Tintor then left on S. Calle Larga. Cross the beautiful bridge with the wrought iron railing and be prepared for an Italian postcard picture.

As you are walking down the streets you will be treated to apartment living Italian style. Ornate front doors with gold nameplates, flower boxes overflowing with beautiful flowers gracing each window; this street leads you into the Italian lifestyle. The walk includes close to twenty small stores, including health food, antique furniture, antique jewelry, specialty bread shops with freshly baked bread, artisans' shops of hand-painted tiles, pottery, masks, pen and ink drawings of Italy, and no sidewalk street merchants. You will have the opportunity to shop with the Italian people of Venice in the Campo Dell 'Orio. Now you are at the end of Calle Largo.

This campo has four restaurants with outside seating. On the weekends, **Trattoria Capitan Uncino** will even extend tables, adding light and umbrellas, giving you the feeling of eating in a garden. Be prepared for the dessert cart—it's a killer.

The gathering of children at this campo can turn an old soccer ball into a full-fledged game on the rough stones of the square. They use the twelfth-century church wall of **San Giacomo** as their goal. Children can be rollerskating and bike riding around parents and grandparents who don't seem to worry about their not wearing headgear or elbow and knee guards. Everyone seems to know they have the community approval of having fun, but the children seem to have a sixth sense and guard the elders from any contact with the many balls, bikes, and roller skates. Balls will be snatched seconds before they collide with a senior who is walking across the campo. The best part of this scene is that the elders just expect the children to protect them!

There is also a co-**op market** in the campo, and if you feel the need to touch base with a "back home supermarket," this is a mini version. A couple of words of warning: 1) Be careful to step over the shoppers' dogs that must wait in front of the store (one of the few places in Italy where dogs are not welcome), and 2) If you decide to buy some fresh fruit or vegetables, be sure to use the plastic gloves available in that department. Touching fruit and vegetables with your bare hands is bad form in Italy.

When you are purchasing fruit or vegetables anywhere in Italy, "don't touch." Always ask for service, tell the person when you intend to eat the fruit and they will choose the ripest for your needs. If this is a self-service department, you will find a box full of plastic gloves.

Churches anchor most campos in Italy. The anchor at Orio is the beautiful and very old **San Giacomo dell Orio.**

➢ **Location**
San Giacomo dell Orio

➢ **Hours: 1000–1700**
Monday–Saturday

➢ **Admission: 3,00 euros**

This church is wheelchair accessible with a companion helping to move the chair up and down the seven steps in the church.

This amazing church contains samples of the most religious architecture techniques from the sixth to the sixteenth century.

There is a sixth-century column that is next to a polished column of green marble that was brought to Venice by the Fourth Crusades from **Constantinople**. The name of the church is said to include everything from **St. James of the Wolf** to the **Orio Family**. The building clearly shows the additions it collected during different epochs.

The façade is **Romanesque,** and you can still admire the ancient square bell tower from the thirteenth century. This building has a Latin cross plan and a central nave, two aisles, and a large transept. Worth seeing is the beautiful wooden ship's keel roof with decorated wooden beams built after 1345. Church art shows the long history of the building from the ancient marble front to the thirteenth- to eighteenth-century paintings. Most interesting are the exterior's bricks at the back of the church. You can see the areas that are used for soccer. This seems to confirm the church's support of children being children. You see no coaches, no police, no equipment. Just soccer balls and lots of family fun.

## Author's Comments

Sometimes you just need a place to sit and relax, away from the hassle, to remember why you came on vacation; it's here.

# Guglie Dock—Ghetto Nuovo and Murano Island

➤ **Vaporetto Dock: Guglie (Canal Cannaregio)**
Boats 41,42,51,52

This passageway from Guglie Dock continues to reflect the warm culture of those Jewish occupants of the present-day ghetto who chose to remain in this formerly restrictive area.

# The World's First Ghetto

➢ **Interest**
This is where Shakespeare's Shylock lived in the play *The Merchant of Venice*. Some historians have described this first ghetto as one of the powerful forces of Venice. The Jewish inhabitants had a special understanding of the total Middle East. This gave Venice an advantage in trade.

➢ **Vaporetto Dock: Guglie**
Boats: 41, 42, 51, and 52

These unique island boats can be taken from Ferrovia (the railroad station). This short ride to Guglie vaporetto dock can be taken later to the island of Murano. This stop is off the Grand Canal on a side canal called Cannaregio.

➢ **Walking Directions**
Walking and wheelchair travel is possible from the railroad station. After leaving the Ferrovia vaporetto dock, turn right and walk straight down Rio Tera Lista di Spagna to Campo S. Geremia. This leads to one of the few large wheelchair-accessible bridges in Venice. Turn left opposite the bottom of this bridge onto Fond di Cannaregio, move by the Guglie Dock to the orange sign with an arrow pointing to the small passageway entrance of the ghetto.

➢ **Admission**
The view from the bridge to the ghetto, its Holocaust Monument, and surrounding area is priceless and free. A

reasonable charge for the museum tour adds to the richness of knowledge.

> **Museum: 3,00 euros**

> **Synagogue Hours**
> Open six days per week 1000–1900
> Closed for visitations on Saturdays
> Guided tours in English are available hourly 1030–1630
> for 8,00 euros

> **Phone: 041.715.359**
> It's best to call to confirm your visit.

### Easy Touring

Leaving the Guglie Dock, one moves down a small passageway and over the Ghetto Vecchio Canal Bridge. This bridge leads to the Campo Ghetto Nuovo. The bridge is an eight-step climb up to a flat walk of ten paces and eight steps down. If the wheelchair riders can be helped over the bridge, they will be able to experience the total ghetto area.

### Ghetto Touring

There are still the remains of a number of homes and businesses built in this ghetto for the Jewish population. These surround the large campo.

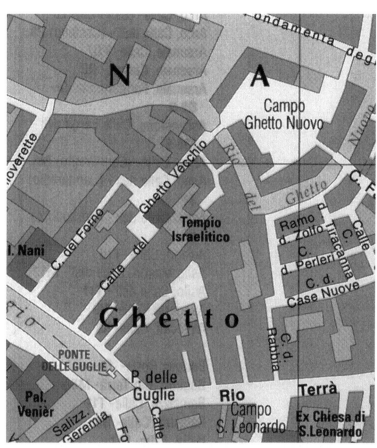

This map shows how to reach Campo Ghetto Nuovo by going down Calle del Forno from Guglie dock.

Originally this small area had eight- and ten-story buildings with small rooms to hold the Jewish community because of their restricted space. The goal of visitors to this area should be to visit the museum and the synagogues. When you have finished your tour, wander around the campo and see a modern presence in this area. It will give you the feeling of the community life that is still richly practiced.

It is recommended that you take the guided tours of the museum and the three ancient synagogues. The second-floor synagogues were built between 1500 and 1650 in this crowded community. They are dedicated to the **Ashkenazi Rite,** the **Sephardic-Levantine Rite**, and the **Italian Rite**. The stair climbing is well worth the effort.

The museum tours spend time in each of the three synagogues. All three show the artistry of the Jewish religious community.

The synagogues vary in their richness but all demonstrate the unhappy fate of building synagogues under the edict of showing no external signs of being a house of worship. The tour guides are excellent, professional, and informative.

### Ghetto History

The word *ghetto* connotes a prison-like meaning in the present-day world. Everything negative about this word becomes difficult to understand until one considers how the Venetian city fathers forced its Jewish citizens to live in the least desirable location, an old foundry. The Venetian word foundry is **gettato**. It easily became mispronounced into "ghetto."

The area at that time was a small island that supposedly provided protection for the Jews. In reality, it provided access for Christian businessmen to the banking skills and loans of the only people in society who could charge interest for loans. Much like the Medicis of Florence, good business could exist only where money could be borrowed. Some writers have described this world's first ghetto in its heyday as the financial district of Venice.

Venice was one of the few European cities that welcomed Jews. They were encouraged to migrate to Venice in 1300. Their migration increased to the point where Venice organized a community location in 1516, providing the land for their campo. There were a number of rules that allowed Jews to practice their religion and set up certain businesses. However, they had to remain in their community at night and travel only by day in the so-called Christian Venice.

The Venetian role as a world trade leader required the Jewish knowledge of the Middle East and their source of loans to conduct trading business. The Venetian Jews had the religious freedom to make loans, charge interest, and give banking services to a community of Christian businessmen.

**Author's Comments:** The Guglie Dock provides access to vaporetto boats … to the marvelous **Island of Murano** with its world famous glass industries. This place had a monopoly on the world's supply of glass products and continues to have a monopoly on beautiful glass.

➢ **Vaporetto Dock: Murano Museo Vaporetto Dock**
 Boats 41, 42

Basilica dei SS. Maria e Donato on Murano Island is said to contain the remains of a saint and the bones of a dragon slain by him.

# Island of Murano

➢ **Interest**
Most of the buildings in Venice were made of wood during the twelfth century. Several disastrous fires led to moving the furnaces used in the glass industry to the island of Murano about a mile away to the north. The isolation of this highly secret business led to the world having to depend on this little island for artistic and industrial glass products until the nineteenth century.

➢ **Vaporetto Docks *to* Murano**
Ferrovia, San Zaccaria, Fondamenta Nuove
Boats: 41, 42, 71, 72, and D.M.

➢ **Vaporetto Docks *on* Murano Island**
Faro, Navagero, Museo, Venier a.nd Colonna.
Boats: 41, 42, 71, 72, and D.M.

**Ease of Touring**

These narrow vaporetti with strong hulls do not have the large flat decks of their sister ships of the Grand Canal. They are extremely seaworthy, but it is not easy to walk about on their decks. They are used to navigating the narrow canals, safely riding the waves of the Adriatic Sea and make the trips to the outer islands. Wheelchair travelers require considerable assistance from the boat crews.

Vaporetto riders may disembark at the Museo dock for touring the museum and Basilica Maria e Donato on Murano or may disembark at Faro and do some walking to enjoy the colorful buildings of Murano.

### Island "Free" Tours

Murano's prestigious glass industry has its plush salesrooms near the Coloma vaporetto dock. If you get off the boat here, there is a good chance that you will be met by enthusiastic salespeople offering to escort you to their exhibits. In fact, you may be offered free water taxi rides to the island from your hotel or other parts of Venice. If you accept these rides, there will be considerable pressure to buy an expensive "artwork" before you can get a ride back to Venice. You can always take a vaporetto.

Murano is a wonderful place to visit. You will feel it is another piece of Venice, only calmer and older. In fact, it was settled before the first frightened immigrants pushed onto the mudflats of Venice. Take the vaporetto to Museo and begin a leisurely stroll to Museo Vetrario, where the mystery of glass is explained, and the Basilica of San e Donato with its bones of a dragon.

# Museo dell'Arte Vetrario

> ## Interest
> This old palace shows that early Murano glass technicians were threatened with death if they left the island and gave away the secrets of glassmaking.

> ## Vaporetto Dock: Museo
> Boats: 41, 42, 71, 72, and D.M.

> ## Location
> Fondamenta Giustinian Murano

> ## Phone: 041.739.586

> ## Hours: 0800–1700
> Thursday–Tuesday (closed on Wednesday)

**Museum Tour**

This museum shows outstanding examples of chandeliers, marriage cups, glass beads, and mirror technology. The archeological section shows a collection of embossing tools, utensils, cups, and necklaces. The museum also contains a collection of modern glass. Maps show where the small independent furnaces and shops are located on the island.

**Author's comments:** The museum allows the visitor to view Murano glass and all of its beauty without the pressure of the sales showrooms.

# School of Vetro Abate Zanetti

➢ **Interest**
This is a glass school, open and fully functioning.

➢ **Vaporetto Dock: Faro**
Boats: 41, 42, 71, 72, and D.M.

➢ **Location**
Calle Briati 8/b

➢ **Phone: 39.041.527.5757**

➢ **Hours**
You should call for days and hours of free tours.

**School Tour**

The school is now open. Although new, it follows the traditional footsteps of one of the most antique institutions of glass in Murano, the Design School of Murano Glassworkers, which was founded in 1862.

A plan of collaboration activated in 2002 between the School of Glass Zanetti Abbot and the Comprehensive Institute of Murano calls for working each year with approximately one hundred elementary school students. You will see students work in vetro fusione and decoration to enamel in class plans. The school consortium coordinates the competition between schools with The Heart of Venice Commission. This new symbol of authentic Venetian artistic glassworks was developed to do away with cheap imitations.

**Author's Comments:** A trip to this school is truly far and above the hyped tours of the sales offices selling glass products. This school is designed to teach young people glassmaking design and to promote the relationship between science and art. If you are interested in glass, this should be at the top of your list of things to see.

# *Donato Basilica*

> ## Interest
> The body of Saint Donato and the bones of a slain dragon are reputed to be here.

> ## Location
> Campo San Donato
> This old church is to the right of the museum Museo dell arte Vetrario.

> ## Hours: 0900–1200, 1600–1830
> Every day

### Ease of Touring

This is one of the oldest churches in the Venice area. Begun in the seventh century, it was completed in the twelfth century. It is an example of the early Byzantine-Venetian design. The outside of the apse shows a remarkable use of multiple rows of columns.

The original church was founded in the name of the Virgin Mary in the seventh century. In the twelfth century, an unusual gift was received from the Greek island of Cephalonia. Saint Donato and his slain dragon were brought to be dedicated. According to legend, four bones from the corpse of the dragon are hung behind the main altar of the church.

A beautiful mosaic floor and golden presentation of the Virgin Mary can also be seen. The building has a wooden ceiling built like an inverted keel of a ship, similar to many other churches in Venice. As you will see throughout the islands, shipbuilders were the only good carpenters and built most church roofs.

**Author's Comments:** This tour can be a pleasant rest from the crowds of Venice.

# *San Samuele Dock*
## Birthplace of Casanova

➢ **Vaporetto Dock: San Samuele**
(The Grand Canal on the island of Venice)
Boats: 82, N

➢ **Sights**
Palazzo Grassi Museum
Casanova Walk to San Stefano

➢ **Concerts**
Chiesa S. Vidal

S. Samuele Vaporetto Dock provides entrance to Palazzo Grassi gallery on the left, Casanova's Chiesa S. Samuele to the rear, and the beginning of the walk to Santo Stefano Church on the right.

# Palazzo Grassi Museum

➢ **Interest**
See art in one of the most immaculate and beautiful palace galleries in Venice.

➢ **Vaporetto Dock: San Samuel**
Boat: 82

➢ **Address**
San Samuele 3231
Campo San Samuele

➢ **Phone: 041.523.1680**

➢ **Hours:**
During Exhibitions 1000–1900 Daily

➢ **Admission: 10,00 euros**

**Ease of Touring**

The building is accessible and easy to travel from floor to floor. There is a self-operating modern, large elevator. Floors are all easy to walk on and bathrooms are well located on the second floor. A key must be obtained from an attendant to use the handicapped bathroom. The stairs are large with strong-to-poor handrails.

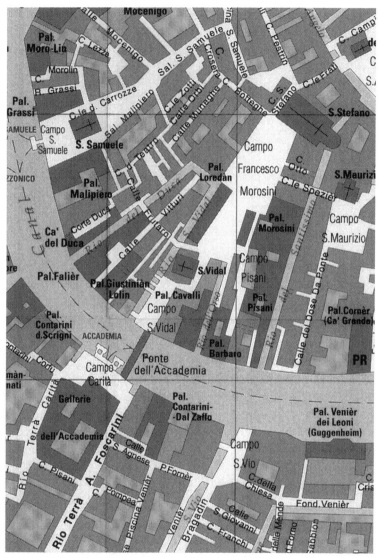

Palace Grassi and S. Samuele dock at the top of the map show those streets leading to the Casanova walk to S. Stefano church.

## Gallery Touring

**Palazzo Grassi, a** sparkling, special gallery, just received an ambitious interior renovation by the well-known Japanese architect **Tadao Ando.**

Its palatial interior now must exceed what it appeared to be when it was first built and occupied between 1756 and 1772. It was designed by **Giorgio Massari**, one of Venice's finest eighteenth-century architects.

The entrance follows several short steps and consists of an easily opened heavy plate glass door. One enters the ground floor with a full view of the marble interiors. The court is a full three floors of multicolored marble façades consisting of a pink and white façade and massive columns and balustrades. The ticket booth and cloakroom are to the left. A well-stocked bookstore is available after leaving the ticket booth. A massive grand staircase reaches the second floor. Two minor staircases can be used on each side of the building. Each exhibit room has a different collection of one or two artists. The experience of just seeing the beauty of the palace is worth the visit. Ceiling art has been well preserved. An excellent coffee bar is located on the second floor.

**Author's Comment:** Expect the best in exhibits in this gallery when you visit Venice. It excels in any subject from "the history of the world" to **Salvador Dali**. It is one of the best-staffed galleries in Venice.

# Casanova's Walk to Santo Stefano Church

Chiesa San Samuele
Casanova's birthplace
Santo Stefano Church
Campo Santo Stefano

➢ **Interest**

No canal bridges have to be crossed on this walk. It is ideal for someone requiring easy walking conditions or using a wheelchair to take a long ride. You pass the place where the notorious lover **Casanova** was born and then go through an area that was once the Venice red light district. Venetian law made the area respectable about the time Christopher Columbus was on his trip to the new world.

➢ **Vaporetto Dock: San Samuele**

Boats: 82 and N

# Chiesa di San Samuele

This church faces the canal at the back center of Campo San Samuele. This is just one of Venice's 222 churches. However, its present-day claim to fame is having had Casanova as a member of its congregation. Vice problems with the local women professionals plagued the priests until they were ordered away from this area in 1500. As if this was not enough of a problem, Giacomo Casanova called this his parish church in 1725. It is still a local parish church that deserves a "look inside" from visitors.

**Casanova's Birthplace**

Leave the church, walk down the street on its right side, Sal. Malipiero. It is on the right side of the church. Look at the wall of one of the buildings, and you will see a marble plaque with the following written in Italian: **Giacomo Casanova** was born in this Calle on 2 April 1725.

His mother, with six children to feed, kept her five youngest at home and shipped Casanova off to boarding school in Padua on his ninth birthday. At boarding school he showed great academic promise and quickly became his teachers' favorite, naturally quick-witted, with an intense appetite for knowledge and a perpetually inquisitive mind. At the age of sixteen, he obtained his doctorate in law from the University of Padua, where he had studied moral philosophy, chemistry, mathematics, and law. He was keenly interested in medicine and later in life regretted not having made a career out of it, although he became an eager and often instinctively good amateur doctor. This man who spent a great deal of time with other men's wives also spent time across the **Bridge of Sighs** in the prison of the **doge**. In fact, he was one of the few Venetians who escaped from the prison.

## The Walk Continuation

A walk from Campo San Samuele consists of continuing down the right side of Chiesa San Samuele on Salizada Malipiero to Salizada San Samuele. You then turn right on Calle Crosera, continuing on Calle de le Botteghe.

The huge red brick church with some exterior décor is Santo Stefano Church. Some **Augustinian Monks** started it on this location in 1274.

# Chiesa Santo Stefano

➢ **Interest**
This church has a leaning bell tower and 500 years of nervous neighbors. Part of the church hangs over a canal. The ceiling looks like a ship's keel. If none of this interests you, there are, of course, beautiful paintings by **Tintoretto, Diziani,** and a glass tree of life from **Murano.**

➢ **Admission: 3,00 euros Sacristy**

➢ **Hours: 1000–1700**
Monday–Saturday

➢ **Phone: 041.522.5061**

**Ease of Touring**

The easiest way to enter this unremarkable-appearing church is through the front door from the Campo. Watch for the rather steep ramp after you have stepped over the one stone step at the entrance.

What makes Santo Stefano different than any other of the 222 churches in Venice?

**Ceiling**

Look at the inside of the roof. It has a magnificent fifteenth-century inverted ship's keel construction, much like the Chiesa Orio. Who else in a city of ship builders could construct something as complicated as a roof?

Also, notice the frescos near the ceiling. Remember, this media of wet colored plaster was the art of choice before the development of oil colors on canvas.

## Apse
This semicircular wall behind the altar of most basilicas was built as an extension of the church's front space. This church had no place to go except out over the local canal. Outside, one can see a special bridge built over the canal to hold up this part of the church.

## Bell Tower
This leaning bell tower has survived in an almost perpendicular position for 500 years. Some of the bells in this tower were purchased from England. Queen Elizabeth I closed the Catholic churches in England during her reign, and the bells were sold to churches all over Europe.

## Sacristy
To enter this special area one pays three euros and climbs three stairs. There are two paintings by **Tintoretto**, **The Agony in the Garden** and the **Washing of the Feet**.

Several students of Tintoretto have painted another painting of the **Last Supper**. The three paintings by **Gaspare Diziani** are **Adoration of the Magi**, **Flight into Egypt,** and **Massacre of the Innocents**. There is also a special glass nativity scene and **Tree of Life** from the Island of Murano. If it's too dark to view this scene, a special light can be turned on and a beautiful effect is created.

Leaving Santo Stefano should be by the same door you entered for ease of walking.

## Campo Santo Stefano

This square is second in size only to San Marco. It contains history, drama, good restaurants, entertainment and even some Italian humor. In the middle of the square is a marble statue of Nicolo Tommaseo, a man of letters and a patriot. Typical Venetian humor twisted the fact that he was sitting on his books by giving him the Venetian name, CAGALIBRI. Someone who speaks Italian may be willing to translate this word.

## The Return to San Samuel Dock

Go to Calle de le Botteghe (the street with which you entered the Campo and first saw Santo Stefano). This will start you back to vaporetto dock San Samuele if you want to return on a walk that has no obstacles or bridges. Remember, follow that Calle to Calle Crosera, Salizada San Samuele and Salizada Malipiero. This will get you to Campo San Samuele and the vaporetto dock.

If you feel more energetic and want to strike out in a new direction, face away from Santo Stefano and the Cagalibri statue and walk in front of the elaborate Church Vivaldi Concert Hall, S. Vidal. Keep walking to the wooden-looking bridge across the Grand Canal at the Accademia Bridge. Cross the bridge to the front of the Accademia Museum. There, boats 1, 82, and N can take you from the Accademia vaporetto dock.

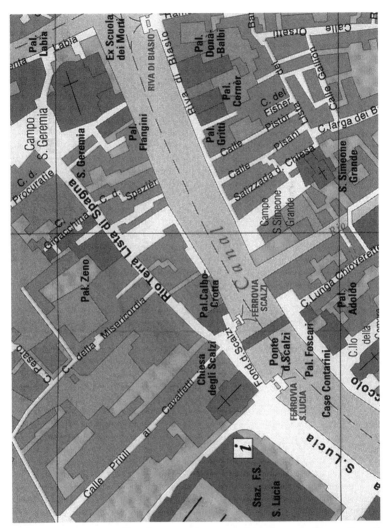

Ferrovia S. Lucia Dock provides an entrance to the railroad
station and S.Geremia and S. Lucia church to the right on Lista
di Spagna.

# Ferrovia Dock, and Stazione Ferrovia San Lucia

➤ **Vaporetto Dock: Ferrovia**
Boats: 1, 82 41, 42, 51, 52, N.

➤ **Sights**
The new Ponte di Calatrava Bridge
SM Scalzi Church
S.Geremia, S.Lucia Church

➤ **Walk**
The shopping walk from Pazzale Roma to Rialto

➤ **Concerts**
Scuola Grande Evangelista

Stazione Ferrovia S. Lucia and Chiesa S.M. of Nazareth as seen from Scalzi Bridge over the Grand Canal.

# *Chiesa degli Scalzi*
## Saint Mary of Nazareth Church

➤ **Interest**

This church has all the sculptures, gilt, polychromatic decorations, and fine marble of the Venetian Baroque style but is ignored by most of the arriving tourists next door at the railroad station.

➤ **Vaporetto Dock: Ferrovia**

➤ **Directions**

Next to the Railroad Station on the Grand Canal at the foot of Ponte Degli Scalzi Bridge

➤ **Phone: 041.715.115**

➤ **Hours: 700–1150 and 1600–1800**

➤ **Admission**

No charge, offerings accepted

### Ease of Touring

Climb past the tired travelers using these three steps for their rest. The floor is unobstructed and many seats are available if you are also a tired traveler. Two steps must be climbed to enter any of the six chapels.

### Church Touring

**The Exterior Façade.** White marble was fashioned in 1680 into a dedication to the Virgin Mother, whose statue dominates the center. Saints are artistically placed over the door with a number of lively pigeons.

**High Altar.** Four pillars and eight spiral columns support the pediment, which is shaped like a pyramid with a crown of gilded wood. These pillars rest upon a pedestal of red and white marble. A small temple with eight small marble columns contains tiny bronze angels. Many other Baroque elements are present.

**Interior.** This imposing church has six side chapels and a treasury. The floor of the nave is red and white marble with several large white tombstones. The floors of the chapels are made of veined marble. According to the cynical writer **Ruskin,** this lavish use of marble was "a perfect type of the vulgar abuse of marble in every possible way."

**Ceiling.** A large fresco by **Tiepolo** was destroyed by an Austrian air raid in 1915. Tasteful oil paintings now cover that area.

**Chapels.** The six chapels are dedicated to **St. John of the Cross**, **St. Teresa of Avila, St. John the Baptist, St. Sabastiano, the Crucifix,** and **the Holy Family.** Each chapel contains its own special confessional.

The elaborate nature of Venetian baroque design in the sixteenth century hides many beautiful single works of art. If one looks carefully at the ceiling of each chapel, the work of **Giandomenico Tiepolo** can be seen. There are several doges entombed in these chapels, including the last doge of Venice, **Lodovico Manin.**

Look up before you walk out of the entrance. You will see a sweeping wooden cantoria (choir loft). The gilt bas-relief shows Carmelite saints listening to music. This was all designed by **Giovanni Marchiori** in the sixteenth century.

**Author's Comments:** Many visitors leave the train station in such a hurry to "see Venice" that they race by this beautiful baroque church. Make this your first stop. It is inspiring and sets the stage for the beautiful things you will see as you continue your journey.

# Chiesa San Geremia and Santa Lucia

> ## Interest
> You may view, up close, the remains of **Saint Luce,** who is wearing a golden mask provided by a recent pope.

> ## Vaporetto Dock: Ferrovia

> ## Directions
> Leave the train station on the left on Fond. De Lucia. Follow the crowds to Fondamenta Scalzi. Travel down Lista di Spagna a street of tourist shops, on both sides, which suddenly open to a large campo with the huge church on the right.

> ## Address
> Chiesa di S. Geremia S.Lucia
> Cannaregio 335. 303121 Venice

> ## Admission
> Free, donations accepted

> ## Hours: 900–1200, 1430–1630

## Ease of Touring

The entrance requires climbing only ten stone steps with four very good handrails. It has one large flat marble floor interior that opens into the chapels. You can climb six steps and walk within a few feet of **St. Luce's** glass enclosed body.

## Church Touring

There is a large courtyard campo in front of the church. Sometimes street vendors fill this area. An old Venetian water wellhead is to the right of the entrance.

The wellheads of Venice recall the days when the Venetians depended upon wells dug down below the surface of the islands. Good water was hard to find until the present system brought water from the nearby mountains.

The interior of the church has a white marble façade and an octagonal shape like **Chiesa Salute** farther up the Grand Canal.

The old red brick bell tower is somewhat removed from the main building by the nearby headquarters of Italian television.

Started in the eleventh century, the present near-circular building was completed but needed reconstruction after fires in 1756. The Greek cross design has four chapels at the end of the equal-length wings. In the middle is a large oval cupola. Every time you ride the vaporetto down the Grand Canal, you see this landmark at the intersection of the Grand Canal and the minor canal Cannaregio. Many superior art items are seen in this large church. It has one large flat marble floor interior that opens into the chapels.

The remains of **St. Geremia** are in a glass casket in a church chapel. The church was originally constructed in his honor; however, St. Luce now shares his church and receives more attention by modern Venetians. To give respect to St. Luce, one can climb six steps and walk within a few feet of her preserved body. **Pope John** in 1960 ordered a golden mask cast to sanctify her face and head. **St. Luce** was moved from her original church, which was demolished in 1860 to enlarge the railway station.

**Santa Lucia's** eternal rest was disturbed yet again on November 7, 1981, when thieves broke into the church and stole her body. The parish priest was knocked to the floor during the crime. A tireless day-and-night search by the police led to her recovery. On the night of December 12, 1981, the **Squadra Mobile** recovered the holy remains of Santa Lucia, and she was returned to the church at the head of a procession of joyful pilgrims.

**Author's Comment**: Tourists are encouraged to visit this church because of its unique design and unusual pair of visible saints.

Calatrava Ponte Bridge designed by the Spanish architect Calatrava shows the new view from Piazzale Roma to the railroad station and the rest of Venice.

# Ponte di Calatrava Bridge

This sleek modern single span walking bridge is currently allowing visitors to walk across the wide Grand Canal from the huge automobile parking and bus connection area of Piazzale Roma to the train station and beyond.

The prolific Spanish architect Santiago Calatrava has finally brought the dream of easy entrance into this fabled city after many years of planning. This sleek, modern structure of steel and glass has brought an expected criticism from the usually outspoken Venetian citizens because of its failure to merge with the Venetian ambiance of classical structures, expensiveness, and the lack of accessibility to wheelchairs.

The city of Venice has promised to provide such accessibility with future adjustments to its structure.

This bridge brings to four the number of structures that span the Grand Canal: Accademia, Scalzi, Rialto and now Calatrava.

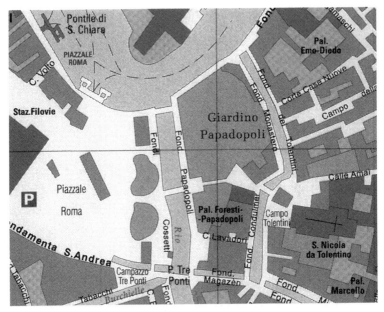

Walk down Fond. Papadopoli and turn left on the alleyway to Campo Tolentini to start your shopping walk to Rialto.

# *Walking & Shopping Tour*
## from Piazzale Roma to Rialto

> ### Interest

Try walking and shopping like the Venetians along alleyways that take you through the neighborhoods and by the non-tourist shops in this old city. The streets, bridges, and passageways of Venice have been here for centuries and will take the visitor by many old buildings and to eighty to a hundred special shops that tourists usually do not see. These shops have a definite high quality to their wares and a decidedly lower cost than those in the heavy tourist traffic areas.

> ### Vaporetto Docks: Piazzale Roma

Boats: 82, 1, N, 41/42, 82, 61, 61/62
**Ferrovia**
Boats: 1, 41/42, 51/52, N, 82

> ### Directions

**From: Ferrovia dock**

Walk across the new **Ponte Calatrava Bridge** from the railroad station. The large parking lot across the Grand Canal leads to this exciting walking and shopping tour to Rialto Bridge, a remarkably short walk toward San Marco. Bus and auto travelers can find the entrance to this adventure near the parking lot.

Start your walk by following the crowds over the large white bridge that crosses Rio Nuovo Canal on the side of Papadopoulos Park.

Walk between the two red brick gateposts with white statues at their tops. After you pass through the park area, you will go under a large pair of white arches with another canal bridge at their back. The name of this bridge is on the building in front of you, Ponte dei Tolenini. Cross the bridge and turn right.

On your left is an old church that looks like a Greek temple. That is where the bridge gets its name. Walk along with the people next to this small canal. Turn left and continue along the canal. Watch for orange signs that say **Per Rialto** or black-stenciled "**Rialto**" on the building.

It is difficult to get lost in Venice if you keep the shape of the Grand Canal in mind. Picture the total Grand Canal as a giant backward **S** shape. You are starting your walk on the top half of this **S**, with Piazzale **Roma** (the car park) and **Ferrovia** (the train station). The middle of this **S** has **Rialto Bridge** (your destination on this walk). **San Marco Square** is toward the bottom of this **S**. When walking in Venice you can't get lost if you keep track of the Grand Canal. Just ask somebody or look for signs painted on the buildings like P. **Roma, Ferrovia, Rialto** or **S. Marco.**

You will also see signs along the way for **Rocco** (**Scuola Grande Rocco**). They will lead you to those special sites; however, remember they will take you off the route to your original destination.

By now you are probably aware that Rialto is more than a bridge; it is the early center of Venice and still has a majority of the shops, theaters, commercial centers, and the huge fish and produce markets—the true heart of Venice.

Just as you begin to wonder if you have taken a wrong turn, one of the signs will turn up and you get an instant feeling of relief. If, on the other hand, you still aren't sure if you are going in the right direction, pop into one of the many shops and ask.

If you have a number counter in your group, let him or her keep track of the bridges—you will cross a total of nine. When you reach bridge number four you are very near **Basilica S.M. Gloriosa Dei Frari** and **Scuola Grande di San Rocco**. Look for special signs on a wall.

This is also a good time for spotting "landmark shops" if you choose to return on the same walk. These might be places where you have decided to make purchases or compare prices with other shops along the way.

**Bridge #4** is also close to Campo Pantalon and a church named **San Pantalon**, a good place to visit and take a short rest.

**Bridge #6** is near **S. Toma** church and the vaporetto dock of the same name. If you are tired and choose not to go on by foot, this is the way to complete the journey on the canal.

**Bridge #7** is near the large **Campo S. Polo** with its church and shops. This is also an excellent place for coffee. Sit down to hear the musicians who frequent these campos. The Church of **S. Polo** is also a place to visit.

**Bridge #9** is very near **vaporetto dock S. Silvestro,** which gives you another opportunity to continue the journey on the canal. But don't give up now, you are very near **Rialto Bridge.** The increasing number of shops and tourists tells you that you are on the outskirts of the Rialto city area. If you continue to follow the Rialto signs, you will be able to see the Church of **San Giacometto** with its huge clock face. Look a little farther and you can see the steps of the Rialto Bridge.

Congratulations! You are in the very exciting **Rialto** filled with all of its sights, smells, sounds, and best of all, you arrived like a true Venetian, by walking. From this point you may choose your trip home. Go ahead to **San Marco Square** using the vaporetto, or test your new Venetian walking skills and proceed to San Marco by following the **Le Mercerie** alleyway of shops and cafes to the **Clock Tower** of **San Marco Square,** which can take another hour or two, depending upon your shopping.

# San Zaccaria Dock—Gateway to Island of Giorgio Maggiore

➢ **Vaporetto Dock: S. Zaccaria**
Boats: 1, 41, 42, 51, 52, 82, N

The island basilica is reached by vaporetto by taking a short walk to the special S. Zaccaria MVE dock and a short boat ride of about five minutes.

➢ **Vaporetto Dock: S. Giorgio**
Boats: 82, N

You can find San Zacccaria church by walking past this statue of King Emmanuel from the dock and down a short passageway.

# San Zaccaria Church

> ## Interest
This church was a special spiritual-political center of the San Marco area of Venice. The relationship with the reigning pope in Rome and doge of the time was manipulated by the members of this church many times.

> ## Vaporetto Dock: San Zaccaria
Boats: 1, 82, N

> ## Directions
Leave San Zaccaria vaporetto dock and walk over the bridge to the right on Riva degli Schiavoni Lagoon Front Street to Sotoportogo. This street is directly opposite the Vittorio Emmanuel Statue. Turn left and walk sixty paces down the narrow street, past the police station to the Campo San Zaccaria.

> ## Location
Campo San Zaccaria

> ## Phone: 041.522.1257

> ## Admission: Free, 1,00 euro to see the crypt

> ## Hours: 1000–1200, 1600–1800
Daily

## Ease of Touring

Go up the three steps into this large church that has huge columns, impressive chapels, and floor-to-ceiling paintings. The floor of the church is smooth and unobstructed. Walking into chapels may require stepping up ten to fifteen stairs. Wheelchairs have limited access to the upper chapels and the crypt downstairs.

## Church Touring

The church was founded in the seventh century by St. Magnus on a small island called Ombriola. A number of tragic fires led to constant rebuilding until about 1515. One fire in the adjacent convent killed over a hundred nuns in 1105.

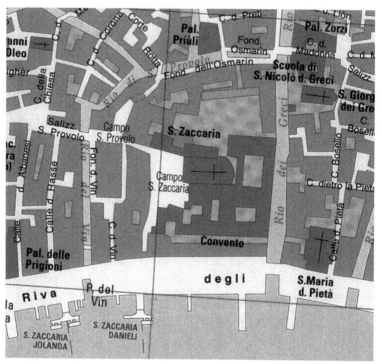

The San Zaccaria Vaporetto dock is near Calle del Vin near the statue of the king. You enter the church from the Campo S. Zaccaria.

The constant rebuilding led to the present grand church, which is a mix of Gothic interior and Renaissance outer façade. The church's interior has a nave and two aisles divided by the large columns.

There is a cross-vaulted ceiling and a hemispheric dome above the high altar. The aisles stretch out in the form of an ambulatory with four radial chapels.

San Zaccaria's importance to early Venice can be seen by the fact that eight doges were buried in the underground crypt. Another demonstration of its importance is the early presentation to this church of the remains of the father of John the Baptist, Saint Zaccaria, by the Byzantine emperor Leo V.

San Zaccaria is still an active church with a membership of approximately 1,500 parishioners. Attending mass in this ancient beautiful church can be an extremely touching experience.

**Author's Comment:** If you have time, visit the crypt under the church. Be aware that it shows evidence of just how much Venice has dropped or the sea has risen.

The Bell Tower of San Giorgio Basilica marks the location of a place of worship that Gregorian Chants can be heard on Sundays.

# San Giorgio Maggiore Island

➢ **Interest**
The boat trip to the island leads you to one of the most beautiful views of Venice. You can see the **San Marco Square** and the surrounding islands from the top of the bell tower. Moving from portal to portal, you have a complete 360-degree view.

➢ **Vaporetto Dock: San Zaccaria**
Boat: 82, N
San Marco MVE

➢ **Directions**
Take any boat to S. Zaccaria station. Exit right and walk along the canal past the mounted statue of King Vittorio Emanuele. This takes you to the San Marco MVE (not shown on most maps). Here you catch the special 82 or N boat to the island.

➢ **Location**
Church of San Giorgio Maggiore

➢ **Admission: Church is free**
3,00 euros to ride the lift up the bell tower

➢ **Hours: 0930–1230 and 1530–1830**
Closed on Sundays

**Ease of Touring**

The entire church has a smooth, well-worn, unobstructed floor up to the altar that leads to the bell tower lift. It takes a few steps to reach the lift; however, good handrails assist you and it's an easy climb. Once you have climbed the bell tower, you have portals to look through. This provides access to look out at the wonderful view of **San Marco Square**, adjacent islands including Lido.

A person in a wheelchair can easily tour the church; however, the bell tower requires someone to assist them to take several steps up to the left entrance.

## The Church

There are two **Tintoretto** paintings on either side of the altar, **Manna from Heaven** on the left and **The Last Supper** on the right. A large golden sphere is part of the altar ornaments.

The art inside the church is minimal. The major benefit of visiting is the view from the belfry and the front steps of the church. If you can take time, it is exciting to view the beauty of the church structure. The outcome is a building of grandeur, which resurrects the spatial emotions of ancient Roman achievements.

**Author's Comments:** If you are an early riser, the church has **Gregorian Chanting Masses** at 0800, Monday through Saturday.

# Lido Island Dock—Cars, Beaches, and Film Festivals

- ➢ **Vaporetto Dock: Lido**
  Boats: 1, 51, 52, 61, 62, 82, N

- ➢ **Sights**
  Lido Village
  Lido Film Festival

Pavement and automobiles replace the canals and boats of Venice on the remarkable Island of Lido.

The Venice film festival focuses on the quality of world films and draws stars to Lido in early September. The world's flags demonstrate the international nature of this meeting of cinema fans.

# *Lido Island*

## ➢ **Interest**

Lido is a long island south of Venice whose name means "sandbank." This island supports many luxury hotels, expensive homes, and upscale clothing and jewelry shops. It is also a reminder that there are still automobiles in the world.

## ➢ **Vaporetto Dock: Lido**

Boats: 1, 82, N recommended on Grand Canal
6, 14, 51/52, 61/62 other docks

### Ease of Touring

Leaving the vaporetto dock, you are on Santa Maria Elisabetta Avenue. Proceed down this beautiful street to experience Lido Island or, if you are there in September, visit the film festival.

### Island Touring

Lido is a quiet, sophisticated beach city. While you are there, you should try to walk the length of the two-way street, Santa Maria Elisabetta, which runs about a mile to the beaches from the vaporetto dock. This beautiful avenue has a garden-like atmosphere with wide, shiny, pink, marble, sidewalks, quaint shops, and restaurants leading to the beaches of the **Adriatic Sea**. There are benches about every hundred yards, so the mile walk to the beach is easy. If you choose not to walk, you can rent bikes or unusual four-wheel (two-person) bikes with canvassed fringed roofs at the vaporetto dock. These are 1960-vintage bikes, so you do not have to know how to shift thirty-seven gears. Just get on and enjoy the ride.

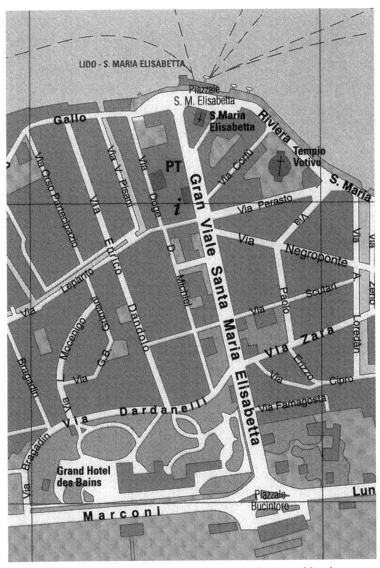

The Lido vaporetto dock is at the northern shore and leads one to the "main street," Santa Maria Elisabetta. The walk past its hotels and shops ends at the fashionable beaches at Piazzale Bucintoro.

During the last week of August and the first week of September, Lido also enjoys the honor of being the home of the **Venice-Lido Film Festival**. This festival does not have the glitz of **Cannes** or **Hollywood** but it makes up the difference by screening some really first-class films.

Lido will give you a chance to wind down from the crowds of tourists and get prepared to return home. This could be a very relaxed ending to your time in Venice.

**Author's Comments**

Some tour books feel Lido is not worth the trip. I found it charming, recalling memories of some of our classical beach cities on the east and west coasts of the United States. The hotels reflect a grand manner, built for patrons who are genteel and expect service with style. Thomas Mann's "**Death in Venice**" is brought to mind in seeing the older hotels.

## ᏃᏃ **The Venice-Lido Film Festival**

Every year during the months of August and September, many moviemakers and fans gather near the famous Casino of Lido Island. Parts of several hotels and the Casino are taken over by the voluntary crew that assembles "worthwhile and creative" films to share cinematic techniques and artistic experiences to improve the art of audio-visual presentation.

Instead of the granting awards to who is "best," the organization attempts to reward the "new, unusual, and important." You can get the feel of seeing many people whose careers depend upon the film media and perhaps a star or two.

The many companies that depend upon this media set up tents around the casino and hotels, offering free demonstrations and services for anyone who is in the area.

This complex operation is completely open to the public. Over 180 films were shown at the film festival one year. Some are shown only for the industry, but the program will tell you which ones. The need for industry exposure gives certain members of the festival priority for seating. However, an amazing number of seats are available for the public. If you are in Venice, you owe it to yourself to experience Lido Island and, of course, the Venice-Lido Film Festival.

Vaporetti reach Lido Island from a number of places on Venice Island. Film festival shuttle buses run to and from the festival grounds from the vaporetto dock. The charge is the same as city bus travel on this non-canal island. Autos, taxis, and rental bicycles are also available.

It appears that regular clothing is acceptable. Most attendees could not be differentiated from regular tourists. Some of the night premiers may require a bit of "glam," but for the most part, "anything goes."

Information is readily available at the information booth. Admission fees run from 8 to 30 euros for individual screenings. Promotional cards are available for all showings over the eleven days for 130 euros for individuals under twenty-five years and over sixty years. Season tickets run from 150 to 400 euros for the festival.

**Information about future festivals:**
Fondaziene La Biennale di Venezia
Palazzo Querini Dubois
San Polo 204
30125 Venezia, Italy
www.labiennale.org

# Informahandicap*, Special Services for Casual and Disabled Walkers

*(Disability organizaton of Venice)

A number of these wheelchair lifts are available to assist the disabled over canal bridges. Master keys are loaned to them to self-operate them.

The goal of this guidebook is Easy Sightseeing. It is for people who want their holidays to be a real vacation where they return home rested. It shows where there are shortcuts, where there are a minimum of steps and stairs, and it helps travelers avoid panicky searches for convenient bathrooms. It tells you where you can enjoy moving from one ancient building to another in the most relaxed fashion.

There are bridges in Venice. Big ones, little ones, and steep ones. On the next several pages, this book shows you how to avoid the unnecessary ones. Venice maintains over one hundred bridges in good condition, and, for those who travel by wheelchair, there are five bridges in the Venice area that have wheelchair lifts that you can operate yourself. Just contact the following information office and request a master key and the list of instructions. These and many other materials are available for travelers who are disabled.

➢ **Reaching Informahandicap service**
   **Address:** Ca'Farsetti San Marco 4136, 30124 Venice
   **Phone:** 041.274.8144, fax 041.274.8182
   **E-mail:** informahandicap@comune.venezia.it
   **Website:** www.comune.venezia.it/informahandicap

# Five Accessible Trails & Itineraries in Venice

The very nature of Venice with its many joined islands creates difficulty for visitors who like to take it easy, have problems walking, or are moving about in wheelchairs. This same problem exists for tourists who have difficulty climbing the high arched bridges when moving from island to island.

The city of Venice has shared the next five maps and itineraries to guide such visitors to the many important sights in the San Marco, Rialto, Dorsoduro, San Toma, and S. Stefano areas of Venice. The services for disabled people of the city of Venice (informahandicap) has allowed us to duplicate the next pages of valuable aids for comfortable touring of the popular sights. **We have retained their English translation of the original Italian with some modifications in parentheses.**

# San Marco Vallaresso Dock— Marciana Area
## Informahandicap, Comune di Venezia

1.  Take the line #82 or #1 vaporetto (accessible) from Tronchetto, Piazzale Roma, or Ferrovia and continue down the full length of the Canal Grande to the **San Marco Vallaresso Dock.**

2.  Proceed down Calle Vallaresso opposite the landing stage (dock) and at the end, turn right in the direction of Piazza San Marco. At the end of the alleyway, turn left instead of right, and shortly afterward, again on your left, you come to the Church of San Moise with its magnificent Baroque façade and the thirteenth-century bell tower. There is one step at both the entrances of the church.

3.  From Vallaresso, turning right you will enter **Piazza San Marco**. You will enter the arcade called Ala Napoleonica. Entering the piazza this way offers a spectacular view, but after the porticoes, you must go down three steps. However, you can enter the piazza without any barriers by following these directions: do not go beyond the porticoes, but instead turn left and go down Calle del Salvadego until you reach the Orseolo Basin. Keep right and you will come to a portico, which takes you directly to the piazza, getting into the arcades of the Procuratie Vecchie. Piazza San Marco has been the beating heart of the city's political and religious left for more than a thousand years, and it is the symbol of the city itself.

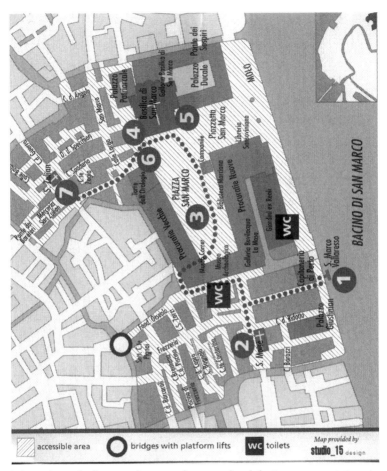

accessible area    ⬤ bridges with platform lifts    **WC** toilets    Map provided by studio_15 design

The dotted lines show where wheelchairs can visit six accessible sights, two WC's and a wheelchair lift (O) without hinderance.

The San Marco Museum Group consists of: The Doge's Palace, Correr Museum, National Archaeological Museum, and the halls at the National Marciana Library.

4. Once you are on the piazza, you can visit the **San Marco Basilica.** The most accessible entrance is the left, although there is a small step about two inches high. Inside the basilica, in addition to the uneven floor, there are a number of difficulties.

   - Access to the Pala d'Oro altarpiece involves four quite steep steps.
   - The treasury is in a side room with two relatively low steps at the entrance, one step on the right and one on the left inside the room itself.
   - For the visit to the museum, you should contact the personnel, as there is a lift to the second floor and two platform lifts, which make the entire route accessible.

5. When you leave the basilica, keeping to your left, you will come to the **Doge's Palace.** The public entrance is placed from Porta del Frumento, on the little square in front of the wharf. Electric wheelchairs for those who cannot negotiate the little stop may gain access from Porta della Carta on the little square flanking the basilica and finally come to the inner courtyard of the palace, with the monumental "Giant's Stair". On the ground floor, there are accessible toilets, a breakfast room, and a bookshop. The first and second floors of the palace, with the Sale Istituzionali and Doge's Apartments, are accessible by lift.

6. Leaving the Doge's Palace by the Porta della Carta, you can admire the soaring shape of the **San Marco Bell Tower.** You can access it by the lateral door by contacting the staff before you visit at +39.041.5224064. The staff will help negotiate the steps to the lift that leads to the beautiful view of the city from above. The bell tower is open every day, from 900–1900 from April until October and from 930–1700 from November until March.

7. **Le Mercerie** starts below the Clock Tower. This famous long alleyway, the most bustling in Venice with its numerous shops of all kinds, links Piazza San Marco and Rialto. You can reach the **Church of San Zulian** without barriers. Inside the church, it is possible to admire the works of Palma the Young. To access the church, you can choose between two entrances: the main one has two steps, while the lateral one has one step. Continuing down Le Mercerie, you come to the Bareteri Bridge.

# Rialto Dock—Rialto Area
## Informahandicap, Comune di Venezia

1. Get off at the Rialto Dock after taking an accessible #1
vaporetto from Piazzale Roma or the railway station. This
insular core of the city was called Rivoaltus until the year
1000, when the name became Venice.

2. Follow the Fondamenta for a short section and turn left
into Calle del Carbon. Immediately before Ca' **Farsetti**, the
Venice City Council premises, is one of the most ancient
palaces of Venice, dating back to the twelfth century, built
in a Byzantine fashion.

    Down Calle del Carbon, you will come to **Campo San
Luca,** where you will find many refreshing bars.

    Keep to your right, turn down the first alleyway on the
left and after a few steps you are in Campo Manin, at
the monument dedicated to Daniele Manin, a famous
nineteenth-century Venetian patriot.

    On the left of the square, you will find a narrow alleyway,
which, turning first left then right, rapidly leads you to
the splendid **Bovolo** ("snail" in Venetian) **staircase** of
the fifteenth-century **Palazzo Contarini,** one of the most
distinctive monuments of the city.

    The snail was built from a round tower and linked to a
five-floor open arcade. In the near garden, you can spot
some well curbs, one of which dates back to the Byzantine
period.

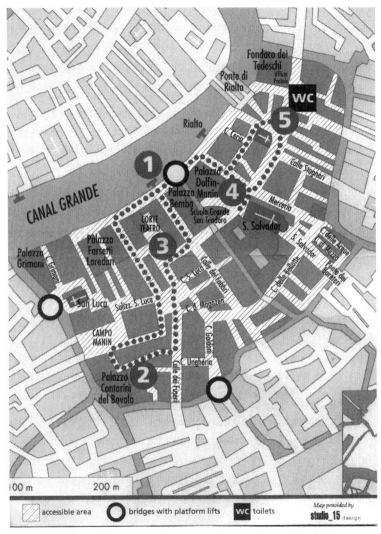

The long dotted lines on this map show where wheelchairs can move from Ponti di Rialto to Bovolo with the assistance of the lift at the large O marked bridge.

3.  Back in Campo San Luca through Calle dei Fuseri, you can continue down Calle del Forno to the Calle del Teatro, which passes in front of the Goldoni Theatre, dedicated to the famous Venetian comedy writer who worked here writing his masterpieces that described eighteenth-century life in Venice. The theatre is accessible to wheelchairs from a lateral entrance where there is an elevator and a stair lift.

    Immediately after the theatre on the left, you enter Calle Bembo, a narrow alleyway that brings you back to the Riva del Carbon on the Canal Grande near the #1 landing stage (dock).

    On your right is Ponte Manin, with a platform lift. After this, you will find the #82 service direct landing stage (dock), and you can visit another area of the city without barriers.

4.  Go down Larga Mazzini until you come to the small **Campo San Salvador** on the right with the church of the same name and the Scuola Grande di San Teodoro, the sixth of the Great Charity congregations of Venice. The Church of San Salvador contains numerous paintings, mosaics, and sculptures by various artists. The main entrance on Campo San Salvador is made difficult by the presence of nine steps. The secondary entrance, reachable by going down a little stretch of Calle delle Mercerie, has eleven steps. This flight of steps can be negotiated with the help of rails on both sides.

    Built in the sixteenth century, the **Scuola Grande di San Teodoro,** besides being the venue for various exhibitions, is now one of Venice's most important concert venues. The entrance to the ground floor is made difficult by the presence of a step, which can be negotiated with the help of a movable ramp installed by the personnel as required. The access to the first floor, which is the venue for concerts, is instead via a flight of stairs with no particular aids for visitors with impaired mobility. Continue down Calle Larga Mazzini in the direction of Piazza San Marco and you come to **le Mercerie**, the famous long alleyway with numerous shops.

5. If, on the other hand, you turn left at the end of Calle Larga Mazzini, you come to **Campo San Bartolomeo,** where there is a statue of Carlo Goldoni. From here, you can see the delightful inner stairs of the Rialto Bridge, built by Antonio da Ponte in the sixteenth century, with two lines of shops linked in the middle with two great arches.

At the end of the campo, turning left in Calle delle Poste you will enjoy an unusual and atmospheric view of Rialto Bridge. In Calle delle Poste there is **Fontego dei Tedeschi,** now the seat of the post office.

The *fonteghi* (fondachi) is the merchants' storehouse. Built during the sixteenth century, it was decorated with Giorgione frescoes. The inner space is accessible.

To return to the line #82 landing stage (dock), go down Calle Bombaseri on the left of Rialto Bridge until you reach Calle Larga Mazzini.

# *San Toma Dock—Frari Area*
## Informahandicap, Comune di Venezia

1. Take the Line #1 or #82 vaporetto (both accessible to wheelchairs) from Tronchetto, Piazzale Roma, or Ferrovia, and continue down the full length of the Canal Grande to **San Toma Dock.**

2. At the end of the calle, opposite the landing stage (dock), turn right into **Campo San Toma** where you can admire the façade of the eighteenth-century church with the same name and, on the far side of the square, the **Scoletta dei Calegheri** (Confraternity of the Cobblers), now housing the local library. The square contains numerous old ateliers and one of the University Institute of Architecture student hostels.

3. Go down the side of the church, and you come to another small square. On the right on the other side of the canal is the gothic facade of **Palazzo Centanni,** birthplace of Carlo Goldoni. The building itself is completely accessible, but you must cross a bridge to reach it. The house is open from November 1 to March 31, from 1000–1600 and from April 1 to October 31, from 1000–1700. Closed Sundays, December 25, January 1, and May 1.

4. If, on the other hand, you leave Campo San Toma down one of the two sides of the Scoletta dei Calegheri, you will come to the marvelous gothic **Basilica of Santa Maria Gloriosa dei Frari.**

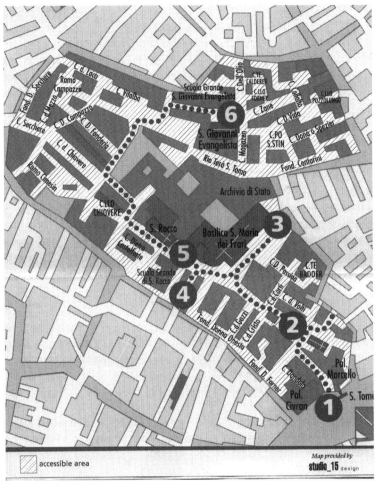

The long dotted line shows an easy route from S. Toma Dock to Evangelista Scuola Grande at the number 6.

The basilica contains works of art of extraordinary value such as Titian's altarpiece of **Our Lady of the Assumption** and Giovanni Bellini's triptych of **the Virgin and Saints**.

The entrance has a step of about six inches, a threshold of about two inches going up, and a ramp going down directly into the aisle. The church itself is without barriers, but to complete the visit and reach the presbytery you must negotiate three steps. To enter the sacristy, there are two steps going up and two going down, but you can ask the personnel to open the door at the back of the basilica in Campo San Rocco. The Sala del Capitolo is, however, inaccessible due to four steep steps. Entrance is free for both the disabled visitor and accompanying caregiver.

5. When you leave the Basilica dei Frari, follow the side of the apse in the direction of Piazzale Roma. You will come to the magnificent Campo San Rocco. Before coming to the church and Scuola Grande di San Rocco, make a small deviation to the left where, passing under a portico, you can admire the delightful Campiello di San Rocco, bustling with ateliers.

Back in Campo San Rocco, you find yourself facing the **church** and **Scuola Grande di San Rocco.** The church has two entrances: there are five steps at the main entrance and four steps at the side entrance.

The scuola contains a famous cycle of paintings by Tintoretto. At the entrance there are four steps, but a tracked wheelchair is available, making both the external steps and internal stairs (with handrail) accessible with the help of an operator. On the ground floor, there is a toilet with a small step, accessible with help. The entrance is free for both the disabled visitor and accompanying caregiver.

6. From Campo San Rocco, continue for a short way in the direction of Piazzale Roma. Turn down Calle Drio l'Archivio as far as the junction with Calle de la Lacca. Proceed down this to the right and after passing two porticoes, you come to the Campiello of the Gothic-Renaissance Scuola di San Giovanni Evangelista, another of Venice's six Scuola Grande confraternities for worship and charity.

The scuola itself, another Renaissance masterpiece, can be visited only during events or by request following telephone booking at +39.041.718234. Only the first floor of the building is accessible (Sala delle Colonne), as access to the first floor is via two flights of the splendid grand staircase by Codussi.

After your visit, go past the delightful marble door and continue as far as Campo San Stin and Fondamenta Contarini, where you can again admire the façade of the Basilica dei Frari.

# San Basilio Dock—Dorsoduro (Santa Margherita) Area
## Informahandicap, Comune di Venezia

1. Take #82 vaporetto (accessible) from Tronchetto, Piazzale Roma or Ferrovia, or #61 vaporetto (accessible for one wheelchair at a time) to **San Basilio Dock** (northern shore of Venice).

San Basilio is on the Fondamenta delle Zattere. This name comes from the timber that was berthed at the quay. A long section to the right as far as the Ponte Longo alle Zattere is free of barriers. In this stretch of the Fondamenta you can find one of the seats of the Faculty of Languages and the Educational Service Library, both of Ca' Foscari University, completely accessible thanks to the platforms at the entrance and an inner lift. The building has accessible toilets.

Opposite the San Basilio stop, go down Calle del Vento and, while covering the itinerary by the Rio San Sebastiano, you will see beyond a bridge the sixteenth-century church having the same name. Going down Fondamenta del Soccorso you will admire the huge twelfth-century Baroque building, Zenobio Palace, which was the home of the famous landscape painter Luca Carlevaris. Since 1850 the building has served as a boarding school of the Armenian Mechitarist Fathers. It is possible to book a visit to the amazing garden by calling the phone number +39.041.5228770.

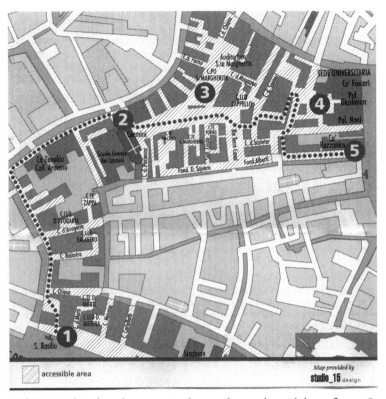

accessible area

Map provided by
studio_15 design

A long unhindered route is shown by a dotted line from S. Basilio Dock past Carmini church to Ca'Rezzonica Museum.

2. At the end of the alleyway you will see the **Church of the Carmini,** dedicated to Santa Maria del Carmelo. Inside, the church has maintained its original fourteenth-century Gothic look divided into three aisles. A painting of Cima do Conegliano and an altarpiece of Palma il Giovane are kept inside. The main entrance to the church, in front of the Campo dei Carmini, involves a step of seven inches. The lateral entrance has a step of two inches. Inside there are no barriers, so the church can be visited throughout. The church is open from 730–1200 and from 1430–1930.

3. Next to the Church of the Carmini, there is **Campo Santa Margherita,** which is one of the most characteristic and lively squares in the city, frequented by a multitude of students who meet there from the various university buildings. There are numerous open-air bars and pizzerias where you can take a pleasant break.

4. At the center of the square you can see an isolated building. Constructed in 1725 to house the School of the Varoteri (leather tanners), it is now the seat of some offices of Venice Municipality. There is also the Santa Margherita Auditorium, part of the Faculty of Economics and a venue for conferences, congresses, and cultural events. The main entrance involves two steps, but there is also a lateral entrance, on San Pantalon Bridge's side, which has a ramp.

5. When you come to Rio Tera' Canal, go down the Calle de Mezo dea Vida. You will soon come to the small, attractive Campiello degli Squellini, whose name comes from the

majolica bowls produced by a factory in this square. You will also notice the near seat of Ca' Foscari University.

6. From the Campiello degli Squellini, you can reach without barriers Ca' Rezzonico, now housing the Museum of Eighteenth-Century Venice. The palace was designed by Baldassarre Longhena and Giorgio Massari, and contains many important paintings of Tiepolo, Rosalba Carriera, Longhi, Guardi, and Canaletto in an environment with precious furniture and household goods of great value. To reach the entrance, go down Calle del Capeler in the direction of Campo San Barnaba, but instead of following the main route, turn into the narrow Calle Pedrocchi to reach Fondamenta Rezzonico. At the end of this alleyway you will find the entrance to the museum.

At the museum's ground floor, there are the visitors' services: information point, ticket office, wardrobe, bookshop, breakfast room.

The entrance is free for the disabled and accompanying caregiver. The museum is open every day except Tuesday from November 1 to March 31 from 1000–1700 and from April 1 to October 31 from 1000–1800. Last tickets are sold one hour before closing time. Closed December 25, January 1, and May 1.

To return to the landing stage (dock), going down Fondamenta Rezzonico, you will enter the beautiful garden of the museum.

# San Samuele Dock—S. Stefano Area
## Informahandicap, Comune di Venezia

1. Take the #82 vaporetto (accessible to wheelchairs) from Tronchetto, Piazzale Roma, or Ferrovia and continue down the full length of the Canal Grande to **San Samuele Dock.**

   On your left is the entrance to **Palazzo Grassi,** an imposing building designed by Giorgio Massari, currently a venue for temporary exhibitions with the accent on modern art, having been bought by the French collector Francois Pinault. Restructured by architect Tadao Ando, the building is fully accessible. The visitor services, including information, ticket office, cloakroom, bookshop, and restaurant-café, are on the ground floor.

   Open every day from 1000–1900. Entrance is free for the disabled.

2. Continue down Calle delle Carrozze, which is lined with art galleries, and you will come to Piscina San Samuele. In Venice, the word *piscine* once described one of numerous pools used for fishing and swimming. They are still known by this name, although they have been filled in.

   Turn right into Calle delle Botteghe and you will come to **Campo Santo Stefano**, at the center of which is a monument to Niccolo Tommaseo, the nineteenth-century Venetian man of letters and patriot. You can also linger in one of the bars in this square, the venue for occasional events such as the Christmas or Carnival markets.

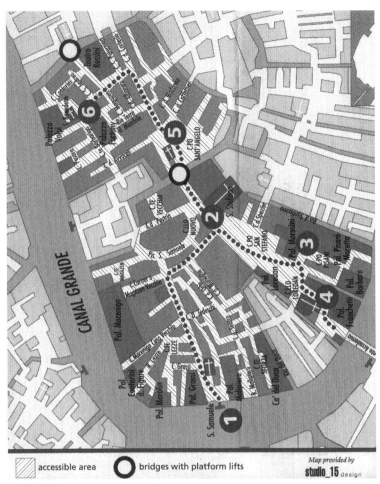

accessible area    ⬤ bridges with platform lifts

*Map provided by*
studio_15 design

The dotted line shows a trail avoiding bridges to a number of sights from S. Samuele Dock at #1 back around to the Accademia Bridge at #4. The bridge cannot be crossed in a wheelchair, but is easily crossed by walkers. The chair-lift past S. Stefano at the O will allow unhindered passage to Palazzo Fortuny.

Here you can admire the Gothic **Church of Santo Stefano** with its magnificent door by Bartolomeo Bon (fifteenth century). The side entrance is accessible after negotiating a step and ramp leading to the interior with its attractive fifteenth-century wooden choir stalls. Two steps provide access to the sacristy, which contains a number of paintings by Jacopo Tintoretto.

The church is open every day from 815–1100 and from 1600–1930.

3. After visiting the church of Santo Stefano, continue to the right in the direction of the Accademia Bridge. On the other side of the square on the left is Corte Pisani, where you can admire the seventeenth-century façade of **Palazzo Pisani,** occupied since 1897 by the Benedetto Marcello Conservatory and containing courtyards, porticoes, and grand staircases.

4. On the same side, the square is closed off by Palazzo Franchetti-Cavalli, now home to the Institute Veneto di Lettere e Arti, a venue for conferences and temporary exhibitions. The three entrances all have steps, but on demand or during particularly important events, moveable ramps are installed. The building is accessible. The conference area, cafeteria, and toilets are on the ground floor and the exhibition areas are on the first floor.

After leaving the institute, you come to the foot of the Accademia Bridge.

5. Going left from the church to Santo Stefano (Point 2), you come to the Ponte dei Frati, equipped with a platform lift.

On the other side of the bridge is Campo Sant'Angelo, named after the church (demolished in the nineteenth century) dedicated to the angel Michael. Gothic buildings and restaurants with outside tables surround the square, a venue for occasional cultural events. From here, you can see the leaning bell tower of the Church of Santo Stefano.

**6.** Cross the square and go down Calle della Mandola, lined with shops of all sorts. Turn left down the second Calle, Salizada del Teatro, and you will come to Campo San Beneto, where you can admire the façade of the seventeenth-century church with the same name and the delightful Gothic façade of Palazzo Pesaro degli Orfei, now the seat of the Fortuny Museum.

At the beginning of the twentieth century, the Palazzo was bought by the eclectic Spanish artist Mariano Fortuny, who transformed it into his personal atelier (studio). It retains the original rooms, structures, upholstery, and collections.

Part of the Venice City Museum's circuit, it is a venue for exhibitions both on the first floor (not accessible due to the presence of stairs) and the ground floor, used for temporary exhibitions.

Entrance is free for the disabled and accompanying companion.

From Campo San Beneto, turn right, head toward Calle Sant'Andrea, and you will come to the bridge of the now demolished Rossini theatre. The bridge has a platform lift and from there you can start itinerary #2 in the Rialto area.

# Preparation for Your Trip to Venice

## What Do You Need to Know about Venice?

You do not need to take a college course in history, culture, or the Italian language to prepare yourself for a visit to Venice. Venice is part of a country that has the third-highest average personal income in Europe. It certainly is not a third-world country you have to prepare for. It certainly doesn't have the cultural biases that you might find in countries like France or Germany where they want you to speak their language correctly. Everyone in Italy seems to have a cousin in the United States. People seem to want to learn English and are very appreciative of your attempts to use their language.

Americans can easily adapt to life in the city of Venice. If you want more specific information than you find in this book about restaurants, nightclubs, and other modern entertainment, you should talk to your hotel staff members. That's one of their jobs, and they take great pride in helping guests.

You should also read some books on Venice before you travel. Look for information that few travel guidebooks include such as, why does the statue of the horse rider at the Peggy Guggenheim Collection seem to be visibly aroused? This is a very special city. Look at the books listed below—they will prepare you to find what makes Venice so special.

## Book Sources of Venetian Information

***The City of Fallen Angels,*** Berendt, John, Penguin Press, 2005. "The loss of the Fenice (Opera House)... was a catastrophe for Venetians, made worse by the revelation that arson might have been the cause. Arriving three days after the fire (1996), Berendt becomes a kind of a detective—inquiring into the nature of life in this remarkable city while gradually revealing the truth about the fire."

***The Courtesan,*** Durant, Sarah, Random House, 2005. The fictional life of one courtesan and her small friend reflects the lives of the many "special prostitutes" of Venice during the fifteenth and sixteenth centuries. A side of life about early Venetians is presented in an informative and interesting read.

***The Mistress of Modernism: The Life of Peggy Guggenheim,*** Houghton Mifflin Co., 2004. "As Mary McCarthy pointed out, Peggy was well aware of the burlesque aspects of her life; she often put them on display. But she also desperately wanted and deserved to be taken seriously. The Peggy Guggenheim Collection, housed in the beautiful palazzo that was her home, is one of the great museums of the art world. Peggy's presence is indelible."

***Venetian Stories,*** Rylands, Jane Turner, Anchor Books, 2003. "In these brilliantly realized, linked tales, the real Venice is revealed—not the iconic tourist destination the city has become, but the mysterious society that resides behind its elegant doors and shuttered windows."

***Venice,*** Giordani, Paolo, Cicero Venice, 2002. "Paolo Giordani takes the visitor deep into the city to explore the traces of the past, at times little known even to many Venetians."

## Internet Sources of Venetian Information

Search engines Google and Yahoo! Perform great public services for travelers by acting like a bridge to foreign information websites that cannot be reached by simply entering website names. I recommend you enter general statements about Venice on either search engine to gather as much information as possible. Use terms such as "Venice, Italy," to avoid getting information on Venice, California.

San Marco Square, Rialto Bridge, and San Lucia railroad station are the three most important centers of Venetian information in Google or Yahoo. I recommended that you enter San Marco, Rialto, or San Lucia along with Venice, Italy, if you want information about those important centers. Other special places such as S.M. Salute will also be guaranteed by repeating Venice, Italy.

You may be able to get your Venetian hotel's Website directly if it is a very famous one; however, don't be surprised if you have to go on a search engine to find your hotel.

# Information to Solve Day-to-Day Living Issues
## Suggestions for Security in Any City

Venice is probably as secure and safe as any city in the United States. Emergency telephone numbers bring emergency medical and police services swiftly by boat and ground transportation. Hotel staff can communicate your communication needs in most situations.

It is of course best to travel with others in any city after dark. The N vaporetto boats have staff that can provide security in that setting. Police are obvious in most crowded areas and your traveling companions offer good, group security. Don't allow yourself to become isolated from others.

A state agency in California once conducted a study of how to protect yourself by your behavior in public. Several psychologists interviewed some prisoners at a major prison to see if people who prey upon others ("muggers") are selective in whom they choose to rob. A group of men who had been incarcerated because of this crime disclosed several pieces of information.

Single walkers in the city can best avoid being chosen as victims by:

- ➤ Walking to destinations with the appearance that you know what you are doing. (e.g. looking ahead without dwelling on the sidewalk
- ➤ Carry handbags close to your body with some sort of shoulder strap.
- ➤ Carry a full sized umbrella that could be interpreted as some sort of defensive weapon.
- ➤ Avoid eye contact with people who appear that they could cause trouble.

## Banking

Call your bank and the credit card division before you leave for Italy. Tell them the countries and cities you will be in and the dates you will be there. This will give them permission to approve charges from the places you visit. Remember, you benefit from any security provision that they enforce.

## ATM Cards

Do not use an Italian bank's outside ATM machine unless the bank is open. Just in case you have a problem, you can enter the bank and have them retrieve your card or give you assistance. Italy's machines are as good as ours but if you have a problem, it's not as easy to call toll-free numbers in Europe. You may also encounter difficulty finding someone who can help you call for assistance in English.

## Credit Cards

Bring copies of both sides of your cards. Also, include the European 800 numbers to call if you need to report a stolen card.

## Cell Phone

In order to use your US cell phone you must call your carrier, say you are going to Europe and that you want to use your cell phone. The provider will give you a code number for your phone that will "unlock" it, and then you can use it all over Europe. However, if you take more than one, each has to have its own unlocking code. The use can be expensive, usually $1 per minute with no free time. This may be well worth the price since it can keep you in instant touch with family, friends and your bank.

## Jewelry, Computers, Cameras

Make a list with full description of all pieces you are taking. Include the appraised values, if you have the information, or the price paid. A photo would also be helpful for the Italian police and your insurance company at home if any of these items disappear.

## Legal Residency

Visitors to Italy who stay more than three months should notify the police of their plans when they reach the location where they intend to live for that long a period. It's not a big deal, however the efficient police forces may need that information to locate you in an emergency.

## Computer Internet Access

Venice has numerous Internet **points, cafes,** or **shops.** If you use email at home it is just as easy to do it in Italy. These establishments range from the back of a little store to large, modern, air-conditioned stores looking a little like FedEx, Kinko's. The 5,00 euro-per-hour charge is certainly cheaper than a telephone call to the United States. It brings you to your home computer screen quite easily.

Some stores may have wireless connections for your laptop or you may have to use their machines. **Be sure to ask for an English keyboard.** German, French or Italian have some of their keys in different locations. **You may have to be shown where the @ symbol is located. It may require striking two keys at once.**

During the busy tourist season you may find the store crowded with students emailing for money, news, etc. Be careful that you do your Internet banking only in the larger computer Internet stores. You may find the bank not allowing connection to your account unless you are in a secure business place. My advice is to avoid using computers for that purpose in small stores.

Once you have paid your money, the time is yours. Don't fret, the attendants will take care of impatient people by ignoring them. Remember, impatience in Italy is not rewarded.

## Cash Discounts

Many hotels and some stores offer discounts from five to fifteen percent for cash payments instead of credit card payments. You need to ask at the hotel when you register and have the cash handy when you pay the bill.

## Electrical Adaptors

Adapting to the Italian 220-volt electrical system is not as difficult as it was a few years ago. Most hotels and apartments have regular 220-volt electrical irons and hair dryers available for your use.

The strange-looking round two- and three-prong plugs can be adapted to our flat two-prong plugs when you are using your own 110-volt American electric appliance, if it states that you can use 100–120 volts. This adaptor works very well with our shavers, laptop computers, etc., and can be purchased at any hardware, electrical appliance, or computer shop. You may want to get one adapter for each unit you will be using.

Check your laptop, battery chargers, electric shavers, hair dryers, and other electrical medical equipment (such as CPAP machines). If these have the printed statement, "AC adapter, input 100–240 volts" or "100–240 volts AC/DC," this means your electrical appliance will adapt to up to 240 volts, AC or

DC with the proper adapter. If your unit does not have this statement or if you are unsure, call the 800 number on your appliance before you leave the United States.

Plan to purchase a transformer for those electrical appliances that do not have a statement that you can use 100–240 volts. These are available in America at Radio Shacks and other electronics stores.

## Street Maps

You should buy a street map of Venice before your trip from a bookstore or www.map.com. This Santa Barbara, California, Website or phone contact (800-430-7532) offers maps delivered by UPS and can have one sent to you in two days. Order the Venice Fleximap or something similar. It is plastic covered and is very clear to read. Street maps cost from seven to ten dollars. **Venice, Easy Sightseeing,** has a number of maps that show the streets and canal in the areas right around vaporetto stops, however you should have additional maps.

## Street Numbers

Most streets or alleyways are like others in Europe. The name of the street may run only for one block and may have numbers running around the street rather than the odd numbers on one side and even numbers on the other.

## Passports

The State Department advises citizens to apply at least twelve to fifteen weeks before they plan to travel out of the United States. (This now includes travel to Mexico, Canada, and the Caribbean.)

For first-time applicants, the US Postal Service charges $97 (photos cost an additional $15). Two payments are required: $67 to the State Department and $30 to the Postal Service. The fee for passport renewal is $67. Expedited processing is available for $189.50 (not including photos).

These prices may have recently changed. Check at your US Post Office.

The department states that 13% of applications are delayed by simple errors such as not signing the application, forgetting to include a check or writing the wrong amount, or submitting a photograph that does not meet the department's specifications.

Duplicate the information page in your passport in case you lose the original. It will save time in receiving a replacement from the American Consulate.

Remember to treat your passport as your citizenship in the United States. Don't give it up unless requested by the police.

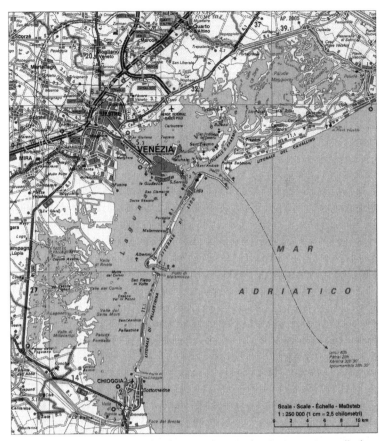

This map again shows the large area in the "Terra Firma" that shares the Marco Polo Airport and leads to a crowded situation at times.

# *Arrival in Venice*
## Air

Starting your trip by air in Venice begins on the mainland, not the islands of Venice. When landing at the airport on a clear day, you can see the many small islands of Venice connected by bridges, with the Grand Canal snaking its way through the hundreds of palaces, churches, and museums. Also visible is a long land bridge, a causeway that carries trains and cars to the train station and Piazzale Roma.

A large metropolitan area on Terra Firma makes one aware that this airport serves a larger population area. Millions of passengers go through its gates on the 700 flights to and from their fifty destinations. Be prepared to land at a very modern, medium-sized airport with lots of fellow travelers.

### Marco Polo International Airport (VCE)
**Location:** 7.5 miles from Venice by land
**Phone:** 041.260.6111
**Fax:** 041.260.6260
**Email**: airportelite@veniceairport.it
**Website**: www.veniceairport.it

The airport serves a rather large area of mainland Italy as well as Venice. Today's concerns for security sometimes cause lines to form during its busy air traffic times; however, it maintains efficient arrival service to travelers. **Venice, Returning Home** describes Marco Polo Airport's departure procedures and time constraints for leaving Venice.

### Shuttle Service
**Phone:** 041.541.5886 or 041.260.9260
This service connects the two terminals, boat docks, and various car parks. It maintains several excellent English-speaking information stations inside the terminal.

### Airport Services
Twenty-four-hour ATMs and money exchanges are available as well as bars, cafes, luggage claim, first aid station, prayer room, and a spa. Facilities for the disabled are fully accessible with available wheelchairs. Wheelchair lifts and ramps provide access to all areas on the two floors of this terminal.

### Water Travel to Venice
Phone: 041.541.5180
The most convenient arrival travel is the non-stop water taxi system. This is about the only way you will be able to take an uncomplicated trip to your hotel with your luggage.

Call your hotel and find out the closest dock you can use. This is truly the grandest style possible to enter the city. You deserve this if you have flown on the typical twelve- to fifteen-hour plane trip and you would like the most romantic and comfortable trip to your hotel room. However, comfort and romance can be costly. Water taxis have no meters so you should negotiate your trip's cost before you ride. Rides are approximately $125 for four people. When you have retrieved your luggage in the terminal, make your way to the water taxi dock to the left of the terminal.

### Airport Boat

Phone: 041.541.4180

Tickets: Purchase in the terminal

This boat takes passengers to the dock at San Marco Square for about $12. Your hotel may recommend that you take this boat if it is near San Marco. Possibly a short water taxi ride will then get you to your hotel for less cost.

### Land Travel: Taxi

Phone: 041.93.6222

Location: Lined up in front of the air terminal.

Cost: Taxis have meters—approximately $35 for trip

These taxis can take you to the Piazzale Roma in about thirty minutes.

### ATVO Fly Bus

Phone: 041.541.4180

Location: Lined up in front of the air terminal

Numbers: 15 or 5

Cost: $5

## Piazzale Roma

This is the large parking area at the northwest end of the island of Venice. If your hotel is near the railroad station, you can walk across the new **Ponte Calatrava.** From here, you can decide if you want to take a water taxi to your hotel or to use the vaporetto. If you have luggage of more than one or two medium-size bags, you may want to take a water taxi. Boarding and managing baggage on the vaporetto is difficult. Wheelchair travelers should send their baggage from the airport before riding the vaporetti.

## Vaporetti

Location: Piazzale Roma

Cost: 6,00 euros, including your luggage

If your hotel gave you the name of the nearest vaporetto stop or dock, take either the #1 or the #82 boat. The #1 dock is to the left. This boat stops at all docks on the way to Rialto, San Marco, and Lido. It is slow, but sure.

Boat #82 dock is right behind the ticket office. It is like a limited bus. It stops only at the more important docks on the way up to Rialto, San Marco, and Lido Island. Make sure it stops at your hotel's vaporetto dock.

Take only boats going to the right or up the canal unless you want a long ride in the wrong direction.

### Internet Additional Information

Google: Marco Polo Airport Venice, Venice Marco Polo Airport
and Venice for Visitors Tourist Information on Marco Polo
Airport Venice.

# Rail

### Stazione Ferrovia Santa Lucia

This is your final destination by train to Venice. Like most
European railroad stations, trains head into the station from
the rear with the arriving trains side by side. This modern
station is self-contained with ticketing services, food service,
stores, tourist assistance, and hotel reservation services in its
rectangular building and two "outrigger" rows of baggage
rooms on the right and restrooms on the left.

Porters will meet each train on the platforms to take bags to
the front of the station. Their service can result in having bags
taken to hotels or just around to the front of the station. If you
have considerable luggage, you should have your bags delivered
to your hotel. Check to see if your hotel provides this service
when you make your reservation.

The long smooth ramp can allow you to roll your own luggage
and any wheelchairs down to the front by walking through a
passage on the left of the station's rear. This takes you down to
the canal's edge, bypassing a large number of steps in front of
the station.

If you choose to enter this gorgeous city with a grand entrance, walk directly through the station and step out of the main entrance. Venice and the Grand Canal are spread out before your eyes in this breathtaking first view.

### Getting to Your Hotel

If your hotel is nearby, you can probably go there by walking to the left in front of the **Scalzi Church.** Other hotels can be reached by crossing the canal over the **Scalzi Bridge** in front of the church. In most cases, you will have to go up the Grand Canal by boat to your left.

### Water Taxi

Water taxis can be reached in front of the station. They are very comfortable with the taxi operator loading your luggage and swiftly taking you to your choice of many hotels, either on the Grand Canal or the many minor canals in Venice. The price of this luxury may be more than your budget allows, but it's worth it for the speed, comfort, and a great trip up the Grand Canal.

### Vaporetti

Vaporetti are very safe and the least expensive of the canal travel. See the **Magic Carpets of Venice** chapter.

# Where Do They Go?

### Boat #1 Dock

(To the far right front of the station) This boat stops at all docks on the Grand Canal. It is slow, but well tended. The boats to **Rialto, San Marco,** and **Lido** leave to the left. The boats to **Piazzale Roma** go to the right.

### Boat #82 Dock

(The boat dock directly in front of the station.) The #82 boats are like express buses—they skip a number of docks on the way to **Rialto, San Marco,** and **Lido Island**. This results in a faster trip. Make sure your destination dock is included in the stops of this boat. The boats to the right make a long eastern trip around the southern part of Venice and should be avoided when you first arrive unless your hotel is in that direction.

### Boats #41, 42, 51, 52 Dock(s) to the left of the Scalzi Bridge

These boats go to the left and take passengers to **Murano Island** and to the east along the northern part of the Venetian island.

### Internet Additional Information

Google Search: **Santa Lucia Station Venice**

Venice Railroad Station—Venice for Visitors

www.europeforvisitors.com: Excellent pictures and an article about station information Stazione de Santa Lucia (Ferrovia) Venice.

www.cheapvenice.com: More information.

# *Planning Your Trip by Computer, the Least Expensive Way*

Travel agents are highly skilled people who do it all for you. If you describe where, when, and how much you want to spend, they can put together an itinerary for your trip.

The major change to this service is that the travel industry no longer partially finances it. Many of the commissions formerly given to travel agencies now go to passengers who buy tickets over the Internet.

## Airline Travel

Airlines have become aware that most travelers use their services through their home or office computers. Individuals and families can now perform the services formerly performed by travel agents and earn their own special discount prices.

Computer owners are encouraged to be their own travel agents by using their computers. Not only can this be a fun, informative experience, it can save you money!

You are encouraged also to use your computer to buy airline tickets. If computers add stress to your life with their beeping and flashing lights, I have provided toll-free 800 numbers in the chart below that you may use to reach airlines. You can still follow the suggested planning procedures and order your tickets over the phone with the airline you choose. However, you may diminish your chances of getting the coveted Internet discounts and special sales.

Remember, if you can send email, you can use a computer to buy airline tickets. Try it—you'll like it!

**Note from the author:** I will continue to offer suggestions on how to use the Internet. Regular users please excuse the basic training that I include to help the courageous beginners. However, I suggest you continue to review this section; I may have some new ideas for you to try.

Here are suggestions on how you can be flexible and more creative in planning your vacation.

There is no tour director telling you where you should or should not go. These sight directions to attractions in Venice should help you decide which ones you want to visit. Your computer will let you decide how you want to get to Venice. (The author is a San Francisco resident and has used SFO for examples. Check the chart to find your own local airport's code.)

**Flying to Venice**
- Do you want to go directly to Venice because you don't have much time? Learn how here.
- Do you want to spend a few days in another city like Paris, London, or Frankfort before you go to Venice? Think about taking a train on this last leg of your trip.

## Choosing an Airline

This simple chart shows the major airlines that offer flights to Venice. It also gives you each airline's 800 number and Website address.

| Airline | Web Address | 800 Number |
|---|---|---|
| American | AA.com | 800.433.7300 |
| Air France | Airfrance.com | 800.237.2747 |
| Alitalia | Alitalia.com | 800.233.5730 |
| British Air | Britishairways.com | 800.247.9297 |
| Continental | Continental.com | 800.221.1212 |
| KLM | KLM.com | 800.374.3747 |
| Lufthansa | Lufthansa.com | 800.545.3880 |
| United | United.com | 800.241.6522 |
| Virgin Atlantic | Virginatlantic.com | 800.866.8621 |

## Planning Questions

- Which airlines land at your nearest international airport?
- Which of those quoted you the lowest cost for the dates you want to travel?
- Which one has the European landing airport you might want to visit on your way to Venice?

## Using the Website

If you have decided not to use the Website, skip this section. Use the 800 number and speak to a person who will help you make your reservation and sell you your tickets.

## Entering the Website

Begin the address of the Website, using **www**. You will now be looking at the "home page" for ordering tickets. There are a few places for you to enter information. The name of your local international airport and its "code" should be used. Utilize the chart provided on this page for your code. Codes are necessary for the airline to be sure you do not get Venice, California, or another Venice somewhere in the world. Click on round trip; this will give you the lowest possible fare.

**Sample Airport Codes** (This chart is included to make it easy to order tickets)

| | |
|---|---|
| Venice, Italy | VCE |
| Atlanta | ATL |
| O'Hare (Chicago) | ORD |
| Los Angeles | LAX |
| Dallas | DFW |
| Denver | DEN |
| Las Vegas | LAS |
| Minneapolis | MSP |
| Detroit | DTW |
| New York | JFK |
| San Francisco | SFO |
| Seattle | SEA |
| St. Louis | STL |

**Typical Flight to Venice (VCE) from San Francisco (SFO)**
**Economy:** $1,900 Fare per Person

1486 SFO Jul 14, 2007       ORD   Jul 14, 2007
San Francisco, 09:30 a.m. / Chicago, 03:35 p.m.

86 ORD Jul 14, 2007   LHR    Jul 15, 2007
Chicago, 05:00 p.m. / London, 06:50 a.m.

6384 LGW Jul 15, 2007       VCE    Jul 15, 2007
London 09:50 a.m. / Venice 01:00 p.m.

Notice the plane changes in Chicago and London for a total flight time of eighteen hours and thirty minutes. Also, notice that there will be a "fare per person" of $1,900 on this round trip ticket.

**Planning Time**
The best part of being your own travel agent is that you are not under any obligation to purchase tickets! Let's leave the Website, get a cup of coffee, and think about some of the details.

- In 2007, the author stopped in London after paying $739 for his flight, spent a few days in London and then took a hundred-mile-an-hour train, for $100 under the English Channel to Paris.

- Arriving in Paris, he again spent a few days sightseeing in the city and took another fast train to Venice (cost $300). This gave him approximately $771 extra spending money by integrating train and plane to spend on the two "bonus" cities, London and Paris. This also gave him the opportunity to catch a glimpse of beautiful European countryside at ground level.

Your computer can be a fun tool to plan your vacation. See how creative you can become. Don't forget, if you are traveling in September or October, Frankfurt is a exciting place to stop over to party at Oktoberfest.

Here is the last chart I will ask you to consider. It is the European landing airports of the five airlines that you can consider as stops before departure for Venice.

## Stopover Airports

| | | |
|---|---|---|
| Paris Charles de Gaulle | CDG | Air France |
| Rome | ROM | Alitalia |
| London (Heathrow) | LHR | British Air |
| | | Virgin Atlantic |
| Frankfurt | FRA | Lufthansa |

Go to a Website again, for a sample trial. Pick Air France, www. airfrance.com. Choose Paris (CDG) as your destination. Click the "Go" or "Enter" button with your mouse and begin to compare prices. If you decide to spend some time in Paris and the flight from Paris to Venice is too expensive, consider that it costs only $300 by train, first class.

Trains in Europe are high quality and very much used. In Europe, you have dining cars, beverage bars, snack bars, clean bathrooms, comfortable seating, tables, and connections for your laptop. A hostess is available to help you with any of your needs. However, best of all, you will have a moving panorama of the beautiful European countryside.

Now, close down your Website and decide if you want to go straight to Venice or make a side trip to one of the above cities. Travel by this well-run train system is a wonderful experience that I am sure you will enjoy. The next section will show you how to order your discount train tickets from home.

**Ready to Buy**

We passengers who use the Internet to purchase tickets must develop something besides the skills of working with a computer. This something is that ministers, priests and rabbis have been telling us about for years—faith.

To take advantage of the miracle of Internet commerce, you have to develop faith that someone will take the action of registering you for a particular pair of seats on flights or trains on certain dates and schedules.

## Credit Card

We all get a little nervous when we have to give our credit card number to a strange voice on the phone or somewhere in the huge void of cyberspace. Remember, these companies have to be reputable with a good credit card service or your bank will not honor the charge! In case you have problems, just call your bank, explain the problem, and the bank will stop the charge. You aren't totally without recourse.

**Personal Note from the Author:** I was able to see sights traveling one hundred miles an hour on a train through France, Switzerland, and Italy. I did it while enjoying a fine glass of wine and dining on excellent food in the relaxed good company of fellow travelers who were also on their way to Venice. All this and I saved money, too; what more can you ask? Good luck with your Internet experience.

## Solving Some Problems of Flying

Flying has ceased to be the uplifting experience it used to be. We can see it's caused in part by the tight security measures we must all endure, crowded airports, and seating that resembles animal corrals. In days long gone it was a treat to just be able to fly.

The **2007 Orbitz Travel Survey** by IPSOS Pubic Affairs Project concluded, "Flying is the biggest source of trip trouble." Wow!

Considering that you are being carried with 300 to 500 other humans at about 30,000 feet, over the Atlantic Ocean, to a pinpoint of land called an airport—tell us something we don't know. Expect some problems with a traveling experience. Air travel is still probably safer than driving down the main street in your own hometown, but problems continue to occur.

Of those surveyed, 40% complained about flight delays (see the hazards of overbooking) and 21% complained about security procedures: however, 46% felt that security should be tougher, and 50% of passengers said, if given the choice, they would take a few more inches of legroom instead of a free meal.

## Preparing for Airport Security

### "How Not to Get Booted off the Plane: Behave!"

A light-hearted article by Beth J. Harpaz of the *Associated Press* gave some tips on keeping your seat on a plane. These are some quotes from her July 1, 2007, article:

"Passengers have been kicked off airplanes or detained at airports for uncontrolled coughing, joking about hijacking, breast-feeding a baby, kissing and other amorous activities, cursing at the flight attendants who denied them alcohol, failing to get a screaming child buckled in for the takeoff and carrying a sippy cup of water."

Here are some tips for getting to your destination (be discreet):

"Whatever you wouldn't do in a church, don't do on a plane," says Peter Shankman, founder of Airtroductions.com, a social networking site for air travelers. "If there's ever been a time in your life where you don't want to attract more attention to yourself, it's on a plane."

According to Alison Duquette, Federal Aviation Administration spokesperson, no one may interfere, intimidate, or threaten a crewmember. "It's completely up to the pilot in command if they want to not allow someone to take a flight," she says. In general, airlines have taken on the responsibility to keep order on their planes. They don't appear to be overly controlling; however, the security people and the plane staff of American and foreign airlines do not have a sense of humor. Words to never, never use include "hijack," "bomb," or any other four-letter word.

## Preparing for Airport Security

Passenger safety is a major concern for all of us who fly. The Federal Transportation and Security Administration (TSA) has the responsibility for overseeing this safety process in commercial aviation. When troublemaking passengers create problems, laws are made to prevent them from reoccurring. The TSA has responsibility and accountability for enforcing these new laws. I'm sure you are all aware of the bizarre events involving passengers who hid bombs in shoes, liquids, and carry-on bags. Enough said: let's prepare for the security check.

- Wear shoes that can be taken off and put back on easily; this will have to be done at security.
- All pocket items will have to be placed in a tray to pass though the scanner.
- Computers will have to be removed from their carry-on bag and sent through the scanner.
- Cameras will have to be taken out of cases and passed through the scanner.
- All medical devices will also have to be scanned.
- Handbags, briefcases, and carry-on bags will also be scanned.

If you have anything that is on the "cannot-carry-on-board list," either pack it in your suitcase to travel with the baggage or leave it home and buy what you need in Europe. Remember, you are not going to the North Pole. You will be going to a modern European city full of all the products you probably use. The best source of what you can and cannot take changes quite often. I recommend you go online to **www.tsa.com** a few days prior to your flight, where all the current security procedures appear; this may save you from throwing something away.

Follow the rules, be prepared, and the security check will go faster than you think.

## Health Maintenance on Long Distance Flights

The environment on today's jumbo jets is as normal as the airlines can present. However, take special care when you stay in that environment for twelve to eighteen hours. Prepare for it by following the presentation that most airlines will provide once you board the flight. There are things you can do, however, before you take the trip. These are several tips that are recommended by physicians and health practitioners.

## Airplane Air

The low humidity in airplane cabins tends to dry out the sensitive mucus membranes in the upper airways where viruses and bacteria can take hold.

**Try:** Stick to bottled or canned water and juices and limit alcohol and caffeinated drinks, which can be dehydrating. Keep drinking. Ideally have eight ounces of water or fruit juice for each hour of your trip. Consider skipping drinks that may be made from airline tap water, such as coffee or tea. Also, ask for your drinks without ice when traveling from countries where water safety is questionable.

## Blood Clots

Blood clots, deep venous thrombosis, or DVT, can develop in the deep veins of legs, especially on long flights. They can lead to a potentially deadly embolism, sometimes days after the trip.

At particular risk are individuals who have had recent orthopedic surgery in their lower limbs and those with vascular of circulatory problems. Also at risk are some cancer patients, the severely obese, smokers, pregnant women, and those on hormone replacement medication or contraception pills. People with a family history of blood clots are also at risk, says Dr. Phyllis Kozarskyl, a consultant to the Centers for Disease Control and Prevention.

Stretch and walk around, if you can, every hour or so. Perform in-seat ankle extensions and flexes, wiggle your toes, and move your arms and legs around. If possible, get your legs above your heart. This is easiest if you are in a first-class sleeper. However, it is also possible in a bulkhead economy-class seat, where you can put your feet up on the wall in front of you.

Avoid sitting with your legs crossed or sleeping for long periods. Ask your doctor about prescribing medical graduated compression socks if you are at risk for blood clots. Those who experience the symptoms of DVT—swellings, warmth, redness of the leg, or pain that is noticeable—should notify a flight attendant. Do not massage the leg, which could be dangerous.

## Germs in Close Quarters

The Federal Aviation Administration reports that 75% of commercial airliners now use air filters that can intercept almost all of the harmful bacteria, viruses, and other contaminants in the cabin. Still, that may not be enough to protect you from the germs of the sneezer sitting next to you.

Bring your own lightweight microfiber travel blanket and pillow cover for long flights, because you can never be sure that supplies on board are clean. Airline cleaning schedules vary.

Wash your hands after touching potentially germy surfaces, door handles, toilet seats and handles, lavatory sink spigots, magazines, or other people's hands. Also, use clean hands when touching your mouth, eyes, nose, or any food. "The most common way for contracting an infection onboard is by contact with an infected surface, not by breathing infected air," says **Jolanda Janczewski,** an occupational health and safety consultant. If you can't get soap and water, use an antibacterial gel cleaner. Choose one that is at least 60% alcohol, recommends **Dr. Christie Reed,** a travel-health official at the CDC. Small two- or three-ounce samplers that comply with stricter airport carry-on rules for liquids and gels are available at most convenience stores and drugstores. Use bottled water, not tap, for brushing your teeth.

### Blocked Ears

Flying at 35,000 feet can cause painful and potentially dangerous changes in ear pressure when the plane is slowing or descending. Passengers traveling with head congestion are particularly susceptible.

Suck on candy, use chewing gum, and keep swallowing. Swallowing helps to equalize pressure. Sips of bottled water also help. Do you have a cold? Ask your doctor if decongestant medication would help. Check security rules for packing nasal spray. Don't hold your nose and blow hard! This can do more harm than good by potentially damaging your eardrum.

## E-Tickets

Computer airline ticket purchasing requires that you retain your faith. When you go online to get your flight reservations you may get only a number like ETKT: VS93212558611 as your confirmation of purchase. Be sure to call the airline a couple of days prior to your flight to confirm this number.

The first time I stepped up to the airline boarding counter with a piece of recycled paper from my copy/fax machine, I expected the bells to go off. I expected security people to rush in, grab me, and haul me off. However, to my amazement, the airline employee looked at my number, entered it in her computer, asked for my passport and credit card, and requested my seat preference! I got a boarding pass and a charming smile as she told me the number of my boarding gate.

Approximately 97% of all airline tickets are now e-tickets. If you haven't flown recently, you may want to have the old-fashioned ticket to hold in your hand. You can get it, but it may cost you an additional $50.

## Coping with Your Delayed or Lost Luggage

Nothing is more stressful than watching all the bags coming up and not seeing your own baggage. Well, it may not be there. The percentage of lost luggage is increasing year by year. About one US passenger in every 150 lost a bag in 2006 through airline mishandling, and that number is increasing by 10% each year.

Some blame the airlines. The airlines have reduced the number of their baggage handlers to compensate for the increased cost of fuel and operating expenses. We may be the victims of the corporate bottom line when our luggage is "lost."

Okay, it is a fact, so let us see how to deal with it. Most delayed luggage has just not caught up with passengers due to changing planes for flight connections, etc. If you are going to be at your destination two or three days, your luggage will most likely catch up with you and be delivered to your hotel. What happens if it doesn't? You may be under the illusion that the airlines will reimburse you for buying some clothes until it arrives. Wrong. They will offer you an amenity kit for the first twenty-four hours. Then you will get $25 per day for the next three or four days. A friend of mine received a long white T-shirt as a pajama replacement with some toilet articles. She did not appreciate the name of the airline printed on this substitute nightie.

Remember, do not leave the airport until you have filed the paperwork for your lost luggage and given the airline a phone number and a complete address where you will be staying.

Also, get a phone number so you can call daily and check on their progress.

In most cases, passengers receive their bags after a two- or three-day delay. However, resist the temptation to pack expensive jewelry in your luggage. If it is completely lost, there is a cap of $2,500 per person without even considering the content of the bag.

The caps for international flights are $1,500 per person and some airlines pay you only $9.07 per pound! So, even if it is a bother to carry the laptop, camera, jewelry, and prescription drugs on board, the loss could be worse than the inconvenience.

An interesting Website to visit: www.unclaimedbaggage.com. You can take a tour at this special huge store in Alabama of all the items that never connected with their owners. If you happen to be in the area, it is an amazing place to find some great bargains!

## Overbooking

This is a practice that occurs in every industry involved in the travel business—airlines, trains, hotels, car rentals, and even luxury liner ships. You should be aware that airlines in every country "overbook" most flights.

Travelers will cancel their reservations because of illnesses and other unforeseen personal events. The industry expects this and uses the overbooking practice to compensate. This practice becomes a problem only on those days that all the travelers show up to fly!

## Airline Practice

The obvious solution would be not to overbook the flight, but this is not going to happen any time soon. So at the time of the flight, when the computers tell the crew that all the seats are booked and all the passengers have signed in, everyone is asked to standby until the airline decides what to do. Of course, this usually happens only to tourist class passengers.

## Auction Time

Prior to loading the plane, the boarding crew holds a kind of auction/buying of seats on behalf of the passengers still needing seats. You will hear over the PA system, "We are offering to book you on the first flight tomorrow. Your stay in a local hotel will be paid for and you will get a voucher for any future flights to San Francisco." Gamblers probably tense up at a situation like this. Other passengers may see this as another day or two of vacation.

## Problems

Personal acquaintances have sad stories to tell when they have accepted such "deals." The hotels have been substandard, and the vouchers have been very difficult to use on any future flight. However, other travelers talk of the fun time had with the extra paid-for vacation days. Again, you are the travel agent; the choice is yours.

## Suggestions

Hang onto your boarding pass and refuse any offers like the one above. Demand a voucher that stipulates a certain amount of money, payable on demand. If you refuse to budge, you may get a first class or business seat; these are usually never oversold.

## Crowded Conditions in Tourist Class

A decisive moment occurs when you follow the crew's directions to get to your seat. If you booked the low-cost tourist class, you were probably shocked at all the people sitting around you crammed into tight seating spaces. You may find yourself sitting in a narrow seat about four seats from the aisle with your knees jammed against the back of the seat in front. The second shock wave hits you when you remember that you will probably be sitting in this seat for the next fourteen hours!

## Consider the Alternatives

First class and business class are available on most overseas airlines. They offer a number of comforts that are luxurious compared to tourist class—wide leather seats, fancy food, drinks, and even beds. However, the price can be five times the cost of tourist class.

## New Classes Are Available

The passengers have complained, and the airlines have listened. There are new classes of seating available, priced between tourist and business. These new overseas classes usually offer an extra three to five inches on each side of the seats, and you may be only one or two from the aisle. These seats are sometimes an extra $600 to $1,000. They're well worth the price. Check the price they offer. If they do not offer what you want, try a different carrier.

The increased seat price may mean a few less souvenirs purchased for friends and family, but your comfort on the long flight will make you a happier tourist.

# European Rail Tickets in the United States
## American Discounts

### Seeing Europe by Train

This section will show you the ease of buying discounted railroad tickets from home by computer. You will see how to take advantage of the opportunity to fly to London, Paris, Rome, or Frankfurt, and then take a train to Venice for a short holiday.

Europe has continued to develop and modernize their passenger trains to a high level at reasonable fares. Magnificent Eurostar trains and other modern trains travel as much as one hundred miles an hour from London to Paris.

The railroads of twenty-seven European countries have joined to offer inexpensive tickets to American travelers in Europe that are lower than they offer their own citizens! It is wise to consider reserving and buying these tickets by Internet at home and taking one of these fast trains, which usually take less time than short airline flights between European cities. Once you are in Europe, you are not eligible for the discounts.

Buying European train tickets is extremely easy from the comfort of your own home computer. All you need to do is to calculate when you are going to be ready to board the train in the European city of your choice. If you have decided to fly Air France to Paris by a certain date, bring up the Rail Europe Website, www.raileurope.com, and start filling in the blanks.

The red, white, and blue Web home page requests just a few pieces of information. Enter Paris (no airport codes needed) in the information slot **From** and Venice in the slot **To**. If you have purchased your return flight from Paris after you have stayed in Venice, check **Round-Trip**. Enter **Departure Date & Departure Time** (note the number for the calendar day comes before the month—this is standard in Europe). Now choose morning, afternoon, or evening. You must make a commitment for the **Return Date & Time** if you selected **Round-Trip Train**, and this saves you even more money. However, if you want to leave it open, just select **One-Way.** Enter the number of people traveling and press **Search.** After about one minute of watching a cartoon of a speeding train you get answers like this for a one-way trip on June 14:

| Departure | | Arrival | Travel Time & Train # | Fare |
|---|---|---|---|---|
| 7:42 am | | 2:50 pm | 7 hr. 52 min.  9341 | $167.00 |
| (Paris | to | Milan) | | (economy) |
| 3:05 pm | | 6:07 pm | 3 hr. 4 min.   111 | $267.00 |
| (Milan | to | Venice, S Lucia) | | (first class) |

## Buying Train Tickets through RailEurope

RailEurope (www.raileurope.com) has its headquarters in White Plains, New York. It has centers all over the United States that sell railroad tickets at special prices to non-Europeans. This is to encourage Americans traveling to Europe to use the rail system. Potential travelers share the user-friendly Internet services of the Eurail Corporation of Unified European Railroads.

Your credit card faith is required again. However, you are dealing with a company based in the United States, so there is less risk. When you get your tickets by UPS you will find the train, coach, and seat numbers of the train you will be riding in Europe. The author enjoyed problem-free ticket use throughout Europe.

The earlier you book your reservation the better chance you will have of a non-stop trip from your European cities—Paris, London, Rome, or Frankfurt to Venice. This procedure is just as simple as it sounds. Don't wait until you get to Europe to make the reservations or ticket purchases; you will not receive the American purchase discount.

This kind of trip to Venice is a bit more complicated than a non-stop flight, but imagine sightseeing sitting in the comfort of your seat, sipping a glass of wine as you gaze out the window at the unfolding countryside. You will go through France, Switzerland, and northern Italy to the city of Milan, cross the water and enter Venice at the Grand Canal. What a fitting entrance to start your Venetian holiday!

## Getting Your Hotel in Venice before You Leave Home

There are over 300 hotels in Venice. They come in all sizes and degrees of luxury. Rooms can cost as much as $2,000 per night and can provide a honeymoon suite with gorgeous furnishings, a bottle of champagne, Jacuzzi, and a romantic gondola trip each night through the most romantic parts of the islands. Keep in mind, however, that a bed and a private bath is about all non-honeymooning tourists require. Generally, people would rather spend "extra" money on other items that go along with vacations.

Do some homework with your computer. Carefully making your reservations and arranging your own lodging will enable you to have the right kind of room and enjoy Venice at reasonable costs.

This book is designed to help you make these lodging reservations by shopping over the Internet before you leave home. You will also receive details about where to visit and live as economically as possible. This may mean forgoing some of the fancier "extras" that earlier tourists felt they had to have in this romantic city. You can find convenient, comfortable sleeping accommodations by spending some extra time at a computer keyboard with the information provided by this book.

## Computer Do-It-Yourself Planning

Start working on reserving hotel rooms two or three months ahead of your trip, if you can. Your computer gives you direct access to the rental agencies and lodging managers of Venice to bargain for deals and prices. We have talked about having trust when sharing information like home addresses and credit card numbers with airline companies and Eurorail. Now we have to talk about this same trust in bargaining for a place to stay so that you can get the most for your dollar in Venice. Don't worry, hotel managers treat your credit card with the same care you received from the airlines.

Several months' advance planning will give you a chance to pick the lodging and time you want to bargain for price.

While you are looking for lodging, don't overlook the many apartments also available in Venice. They cost less per day than many hotels and can save you money because you won't have to dine out three times per day. See the section called **The Economy of Apartments** about how you can book an apartment like a hotel room before you leave home. Everyone in the world seems to want to go to Venice, so get a head start!

## Shopping from Home

You start the process with key words on Google or Yahoo!

Type: **Venice, Italy, Hotels and Apartments.** Then enter **search,** and you will see the many places to reserve hotel rooms and apartments. They can all be rented in Venice. Apartments also offer savings in preparing meals and the possibility of meeting Venetian friends to assist you in finding good food and knowledge about Venice. You can book your lodging from home by either computer or telephone.

## Needed Hotel Information

Your search will consist of looking at Websites recommended by the search engines, **Google** and **Yahoo.** These Websites show beautiful pictures of the lobby and hotel rooms. Venetian hotel managers are masters at creating beautiful hotel rooms. However, you need more information.

When you are in a restaurant with other tourists, you may continually hear the following complaints: "I had to walk about a half a mile from the canal to get to my hotel." Or, "I have to climb fifty-five steps every time I go to my hotel room." You need to look for information that will prevent those problems from affecting you.

One of the most important options you can find on hotel Websites is **location**. By clicking **map** you should be given where the hotel is located.

Look where the hotel is on the Grand Canal or a nearby alleyway. If it is on the Grand Canal, you can usually ride the water taxis right to the hotel.

If it is not on the Grand Canal, is it on a smaller canal? How far will you need to walk each time you go to your hotel? Next, in what part of Venice do you want to stay?

### San Marco Square

Do you want to stay near the important tourist sites like **San Marco Basilica**? Enter **Venice Hotels, San Marco** on your search engine. You will see over forty-two hotels ranging from five- to two-star to choose from with a listing of mailing addresses, Websites, telephone numbers, and possibly email addresses.

## San Lucia Railroad Station (Ferrovia)

If you want to be at the other end of the Grand Canal you should enter **San Lucia Ferrovia, Venice,** or **Venice Hotels Ferrovia.** This will give you information in general about Venice and approximately twenty-eight four- to one-star hotels to investigate. This area will be close to land taxis and buses to **Marco Polo Airport**, and the large parking buildings for your car at **Piazzale Roma.** These hotels are excellent and this area does not fit the stereotypical "bad neighborhood" of railroad stations.

## Make Reservations with Care

At some point after looking at several favorite locations you may be tempted to make your reservations based upon the first price you are given. Most people want to get on with other plans.

Look at the sample hotels on the next several pages, and at at other information you should know.

- Where is the room located in the building?
- How many stairs are you going have to climb?
- Is there an elevator?
- How far to the nearest water taxi or vaporetto dock?
- Where is the dining room for breakfast?

European floors start on the ground floor with the first floor located on what would be our American second floors. The third floor is, in reality, up on the fourth floor. It can be a long climb if there is no elevator and you are carrying luggage.

Do they have an elevator from the ground floor? Some hotels in Venice have their lobbies on the third floor. So you may have to walk from the ground floor to the lobby, then elevator on up to your room.

## Pre-Reservation Advice

You should plan on digging a little deeper into the information by email before you make the reservation commitment. Making a reservation is easy; changing is not quite so easy.

- The email message will allow you ask certain specific questions to the hotel staff. The email address is usually located on the hotel's Web site. If it is not shown, try this: Info@*(type the name of hotel's Website)*.
- I recommend that you avoid hotels that you cannot reach by email. You need that information source, and most hotels are happy to give you the information you want.
- Remember the six- to eight-hour difference in time between America and Venice. If you can, locate two or three hotels that you like and start asking them all questions by email.

- You will have to allow a day or so for your answers. Ask a number of questions in the email and start to narrow down the selected number as you go.

- Be specific with your questions. "What vaporetto dock are you near?" "Do you have an elevator to the ground floor?" "How many stair steps is the room from the ground floor?" "How much do you discount for cash payments?" (Managers are eager to save the cost of credit card transactions and are happy to pass those 10–15% savings to their customers.)

## Hotel Examples

I have included descriptions of some hotels that I am personally acquainted with in Venice. These are reasonably priced rooms with double beds and private baths, and are clean and attractive.

Notice the range in prices. Almost every hotel in Venice has luxury rooms available as well as reasonably priced ones. Look for the practical elements of location, comfort, and stair climbing. I have included the information I found that I feel matches the questions you may have about picking a hotel.

## Bargaining for the Best Price

Italians love to bargain. Don't be shy—it is expected and most Italians love the process. Before the euro, Americans were thought to be so wealthy they didn't need to bargain. Times have changed, and the honored practice of American price negotiation is alive and well. Email presents many opportunities for practicing this custom.

## Room Price

Most hotel directories or Websites of hotels in Venice will describe their room prices within a range—for example: 80–250 euros. Rooms have different prices depending on the number of bells and whistles they include. How close is it to the ground floor, is the room plain and the bath and toilet shared, or is it luxurious, including Champagne breakfasts with a Jacuzzi and romantic gondola rides?

## Breakfast

Many hotels provide breakfast. Some are included in the price, and others are extra and can be as much as 25,00 euros per morning, depending on how elaborate.

## Location

How far is the building from transportation? How long a walk must you take with your luggage from a water taxi or vaporetto dock? How far is the hotel from major attractions in Venice?

Read the following descriptions of the hotels listed. The descriptions are short; however, they can give you a start in your search for the kind of hotel you want for your stay in

Venice. Ask your questions by email; you will get the answers you need.

If you find a gem of a hotel, please to share it on the author's Website: www.easytravelbooks.com. He is always looking for good deals in lodging. Good luck!

# Hotel and Apartment Samples

## Hotel Antigo Trovatore

➢ **Vaporetto Dock: San Zaccaria**

Boats: 1, 6, 14, 20, 41, 42, 51, 52, 71, 72, 82, N

➢ **Location**

Calle delle Rasse 4534, San Marco 30124, Venice (near San Marco)

➢ **Phone: 041.522.4611 / Fax: 041.522.7870**
Email: antigo@libero.it
Website: www.antigotrovatore.it

➢ **Cost**
110 euros Db/bath
Most credit cards accepted.

This hotel is a short distance from the Doge's Palace and San Marco Basilica. It is located 150 yards down the street called Calle delle Rasse from S. Zaccaria vaporetto dock. Its ground floor entrance contains twenty-two stairs to reach the lobby on the first floor. An elevator takes guests from the lobby up to the residential rooms. Breakfast is extra.

## Hotel Albergo Doni

➢ **Vaporetto Dock: S. Zaccaria**

Boats: 1, 6, 14, 20, 41, 42, 51, 52, 71, 72, 82, N

➤ **Location**
S. Zaccaria 4656 (near San Marco), Venice 30122

➤ **Phone: 041.422.4257 / Fax: 041.522.4267**
Email: albergodoni@libero.it
Website: None

➤ **Cost**
90,00 euros Db/bath, breakfast included.
Most credit cards accepted.

This hotel is near the attractions of San Marco Square. It is located about 1,000 yards from the nearest vaporetto dock, San Zaccaria.

The lobby is reached by fifteen stairs from the front entrance. It has twelve rooms on its three floors. Rooms on the top floor would take at least sixty stairs to reach. There is no elevator.

## Hotel Antiche Figure

➤ **Vaporetto Dock: Ferrovia**
Boats: 1, 41, 42, 51, N, 71, 72, 82, G2

➤ **Location**
Santa Croce
Simeon Piccolo, 686/A-687
30135 Venezia

> **Phone: 041.275.9486 / Fax: 041.275.6640**
Email: info@hotelantichefigure.it
Website: www.hotelantichefigure.it

> **Cost**
80,00–320,00 euros, breakfast not included

Directly across the Grand Canal from the railroad station. It has an elevator, indoor and outdoor dining areas. Lobby and bar are on the ground floor. Apartment rental service office available.

The hotel is in the middle of the tourist crowd; however, one can walk about a half block to a quiet lane of shops. Rooms are air conditioned, and most have both showers and tubs. The staff is friendly and ready to answer questions to help you make your stay stress free and fun.

## Hotel Casa Fontana

> **Vaporetto Dock: San Zaccaria**
Boats: 1, 6, 14, 20, 41, 42, 51, 52, 71, 72, 82, N

> **Location**
Castello
Campo San Provolo 4701
Venice 30122

> **Phone: 041.522.0579 / Fax: 041.523.1040**
Email: info@hotelfontana.it
Website: www.hotelfontana.com

> **Cost**
80,00–170,00 euros Db/bath, breakfast included.
Most credit cards accepted.

Located near the tourist attractions of San Marco Square.
Approximately one hundred yards from the San Zaccaria
vaporetto dock.

Lobby on the ground floor. There are twenty-nine stairs
from the lobby to the first floor residential rooms. There is
no elevator.

## Hotel Doge

> **Vaporetto Dock: R.D. Biasio**
Boat: 1

> **Location**
S. Croce. 1222 Lista Vechia dei Bari (near Railroad
Station)
Venice 30133

> **Phone: 041.717.212 / Fax: 041.716693**
Email: hoteldoge@libero.it
Website: www.albergodoge.com

> **Cost**
60,00–200,00 euros Db/bath, breakfast included.
Most credit cards accepted.

This quaint hotel is away from the hustle and bustle of the
tourist crowds. It is near the Scalzi Bridge and San Simone
Profeta Church. Walk straight until you can turn, cross a
small canal bridge, then on to Lista dei Bari.

Lobby on ground floor. Ten residential rooms are up twenty stairs above the lobby. The Campo di San Giacomo dell'Orio is located a few blocks away and represents a marvelous native Venetian small community. There is no elevator.

## Hotel Gallini

➤ **Vaporetto Dock S. Angelo**
Boats: 1, 82

➤ **Location**
San Marco
3673 Calle Della Verona
Venice, 30124

➤ **Phone: 041.520.4515 / Fax: 041.520.9103**
Email: hgallini@tin.it
Website: www.hotelgallini.it

➤ **Cost**
78,00–177,00 euros Db/bath, breakfast included.
Most credit cards accepted.

Located about 50 yards from La Fenice Opera House and about 300 yards from attractions of San Marco Square. The entrance is about 300 yards from the vaporetto dock. The lobby is located on the ground floor with fifteen stairs to the residential rooms on the first floor. There is no elevator.

# Hotel Locanda Ai Santi Apostoli

> **Vaporetto Dock: Ca'D'Oro**
  Boat: 1

> **Location**
  Cannaregio, SS Apostoli, 4391/AVenice 30131

> **Phone: 041.521.2612 / Fax: 041.521.2611**
  Email: disantia@tin.it
  Website: www.veneziasi.it

> **Cost**
  90,00–280,00 euros Db/bath, breakfast included.
  Most credit cards accepted.

This is a pleasant hotel located about 300 yards from the vaporetto dock, near the church SS Apostoli. The entrance is through a courtyard garden. The lobby is on the third floor, can be reached by elevator, which stops at this point.

# Hotel Marin

> **Vaporetto Dock: Ferrovia**
  Boats 1, 41, 42, 51, 52, N 71, 72, 82, G2

> **Location**
  S. Croce Ramo delle chiovere 670/b
  Venice 30135

> **Phone: 041.718.022 / Fax: 041.721.485**
  Email: htlmarin@gpnet.it
  Website: www.albergomarin.it

> ## Cost
60,00–110,00 euros
Most credit cards accepted.

Walk over bridge in front of Ferrovia Station. Turn right along the canal and then left at the left side of the domed church, and walk along the right side to the rear to Ramo delle Chiovere.

This is a small family-owned hotel away from the roar of the tourist crowds, one hundred yards behind the large cathedral on the Grand Canal. The lobby, several residential rooms, and the dining room are located on the ground floor. No elevator. Near laundromat, post office, and Internet point.

## Hotel Pantalon

> ### Vaporetto Dock: S. Toma
Boats: 1, 82, N

> ### Location
3942 Dorsoduro, Crosera San. Pantalon
Venice 30123

> ### Phone: 041.710.896 / Fax: 041.718.683
Email: hotelpantalon@iol.it
Website: www.hotelpantalon.com

> ### Cost
80,00–250,00 euros Db/bath, breakfast included.
Most credit cards accepted.

This hotel is near two of the most popular tourist sites in Venice, Basilica dei Frari and Scuola Grande San Rocco.

It's about 300 yards from the vaporetto dock. The Pantalon Church is also nearby. The lobby of the hotel is on the ground floor with no elevator. There are sixteen steps from the lobby to the first floor and another sixteen to the remainder of the fifteen rooms.

## Hotel S. Moise

➤ **Vaporetto Dock: Vallaresso, S. Marco**
Boat #1, 82, N

➤ **Location**
Piscina S. Moise
2058 San Marco, Venice 30124

➤ **Phone: 041.520.3755 / Fax: 041.521.0670**
Email: info@sanmoise.it
Website: www.sanmoise.it

➤ **Cost**
85,00–390,00 euros Db/bath, breakfast included.
Most credit cards accepted.

Located about a hundred yards from the vaporetto dock, near the many attractions of San Marco Square. San Moise Church is nearby with its gondola highway interchange to keep you entertained. Husbands may temporarily lose track of their mates with the many upscale fashion stores nearby. Lobby is on the ground floor, no elevator, and eighteen stairs to the residential rooms above.

# Hotel Vecellio

> ## Vaporetto Dock: Fondamenta Nuove (north side of Venice Island)
> Boats: 41, 42, 51, and 52

> ## Location
> Cannaregio 5039/B
> Venice, 30131

> ## Phone: 041.523.8743 / Fax: 041.277.0230
> Email: info@hotelvecellio.com
> Website: www.hotelvecellio.com

> ## Cost
> 60,00–230,00 euros, Db/bath, breakfast included.

This is a different experience on the quieter north side of Venice Islands. It is a small hotel of nine rooms with the plush decor of the big hotels near San Marco Square. Guests can walk to the Rialto Bridge and San Marco through the quaint back alleyways of the Cannaregio in about forty-five minutes, allowing for shopping.

There are eight rooms on the ground floor of this hotel after fifteen stairs. One accessible room is located near the lobby on the ground floor. Walk out the front door to the vaporetto dock. The hotel is managed by Matteo, a native Venetian well versed in the best places for food, shopping, and nightlife. There is no elevator.

## Hotel Violino D'Oro

> **Vaporetto Dock: Ca'D'Oro**
> Boats 1, N

> **Location**
> San Marco, Corte Barozzi 2091
> Venice, 30135

> **Phone: 041.277.0841 / Fax: 041.277.1001**
> Email: violinodoro@violinodoro.com
> Website: www.violinodoro.com

> **Cost**
> 60,00–320,00 euros Bb/bath, breakfast included.
> Most credit cards accepted.

This hotel is about 300 yards from the vaporetto dock, and there are a few steps to the lobby. However, an alternative entrance has a ramp for wheelchairs. All floors can be reached by elevator.

### The Economy of Apartments

Apartments offer another special lifestyle in Venice. Hotels rooms are great but they are small and you have to depend upon all meals at restaurants. The biggest disadvantage they have is not giving you the opportunity of getting together with the Italian families of the neighborhood. Meeting the people of Venice can be a very rewarding experience.

**Apartments** can be all the way from a luxurious three-bedroom, two-bath unit with a living room, dining room, and kitchen, to a small studio apartment at the other end of the scale.

**Studio Apartments** offer the same home-like atmosphere of the larger units with, of course, limited space. Be it a large apartment or a studio apartment, you will be in with Venetian neighbors. You may meet them in the building, campos, at stores, coffee bars, and bakeries. Feel free to ask your neighbors about the best places to shop; they may even invite you to go with them on one of their shopping trips.

## Hotel-Owned Apartments

The convenience of hotel-owned apartments can be a help to the first-time renter. The hotel will usually accept your credit card, and if a problem comes up with any of the working amenities, the hotel maintenance department is only a phone call away. You also have the convenience of booking your accommodations through a front desk operation.

## Privately Owned Apartments

These apartments are usually handled by some kind of Website agency manager who acts on behalf of the owner. It may take you more time to negotiate an agreement. It usually leads to a renter sending a deposit by wire transfer from his or her bank to the owner's bank.

1. The agency or owner will give you his or her bank's name, wiring number, address, and the name of the account holder.

2. Give your bank all this information to complete the transfer. Your bank may waive the fee if you have special features on your account or credit cards.

**Personal note from the author:** I changed my mind on a certain property, asked for my deposit, and it was promptly wired back to my account.

Remember, apartments cost only about one-half the price of a three-star hotel. But again, you are your own travel agent and the decision of lodging is up to you.

### Local Agencies

Most rental agencies in Venice are regulated, so the picture and conditions that are described on the Website will be true. Apartments can be rented for as little as three days. However, it is recommended that you deal with hotel-owned apartments in this case. But, if you and your family or group consist of six to ten people, the apartment will a considerable cost savings.

### Things to Know

Prices for groups are sometimes quoted in terms of 50,00 to 80,00 euros per night **per person** for seven days. The price will be lower if it is for two weeks. See the sample apartment at the Website www.viewsonvenice.com to see how much a studio apartment would probably cost for two. It is, of course, important that both parties understand the exact cost.

## Hotel-Owned Apartment Agencies

| | |
|---|---|
| Dimora Venezuiana | www.dimoraveneziana.com |
| Magica Venezia | www.magicavenezia.com |
| Views on Venice | www.viewsonvenice.com |

## Privately Owned Apartment Agencies

| | |
|---|---|
| Casseleria | www.interflats.com |
| Vacation Rentals by Owners | www.vrbo.com |
| Venice Tourism | www.turismoveezia.it |

## Studio Apartment (sample)

www.viewsonvenice.com

### Description

Location: Dorsoduro Frari

Ground Floor

Sleeps: 2

1 double bed

Microwave, dishwasher, washing machine, iron, TV,

air-conditioning, shower, children not allowed, no pets, no smokers.

Vaporetto stop: S.Toma

Rental Deposit: 40%

Security Deposit: Euro 0

A stylish studio apartment in the Dorsoduro on two floors (bedroom is upstairs) in the Frari area. Rental price includes gas, electricity, linen, and final cleaning.

Property Rates: 150 euros for 2

# Going Home in Style from Venice

There may have been some complications in reaching your hotel or apartment when you arrived in Venice at the **Marco Polo Airport** or the **Santa Lucia Railroad Station**. It is hoped that the experience was good. Now you should recall how you traveled to your hotel room. If that is the way that you wish to reach your plane or train, just reverse the process and hope your experience will be as pleasant.

### Complicating Factors

If you are flying from **Marco Polo Airport,** there are several problems that seem to appear at any airport.

- All departing flights to the United States seem to be from 7:00 to 10:00 a.m. If you plan to go to the airport by land, you will find that Piazzale Roma has many other travelers trying to catch cabs or buses at the same time. That, of course, means that you have to add up the time it will take to travel from your hotel, check in at your airline on the second floor of the terminal, and allow for security procedures before takeoff time.

# Airport Departures

### Water Taxis

These expensive boats provide the quickest and most comfortable way to leave Venice. However, if you have an early morning flight, make a reservation. Taxi operators are very dependable if you or your hotel contacts a specific taxi driver.

### Land Travel to Airport

Piazzale Roma is extremely busy in the morning. Crowds from the railroad station will be crossing over the Ponte Calatrava Bridge. Buses are full and cabs are invisible. If your plane takes off after noon, there is usually space on buses and cabs. A vaporetto or water taxi to Rome can get you to land transportation in time for afternoon or night planes; morning planes can be handled another way.

### Airport Hotels

It is suggested that you move to a hotel in the **Tessera** area near **Marco Polo Airport** on the afternoon before you leave if your plane takes off before noon the next day. There are many fine hotels that provide shuttle service to the airport early in the morning. **The Fly Hotel** is easy to recall because of its unusual name and restaurant. Many others can be found before you leave home by going on Google or Yahoo.

## Departing Marco Polo

The departure terminal is located on the second floor. The many airline desks can be easily seen and coordinated with their large electronic flight information boards. Getting the boarding pass will be your primary concern. To make this frenzied period easiest for you and your companions, consider these areas.

## Luggage for Flight Home

This is an all-encompassing term describing **Things** that you took on your trip: clothes, equipment such as camera and laptop computers, medications, children's toys, etc. It also describes things you bought such as souvenirs, clothing, jewelry, etc., etc. Just consider everything you have to put inside a bag or suitcase as luggage and you will be able to manage the security process.

## Airline Limits

Airlines will weigh your luggage prior to boarding. You will need to deal with security items that are forbidden such as liquid medications and beauty ointments. You may see fellow passenger throwing items in the nearest trash containers in the airport. That may be your fate also if you haven't checked your luggage. By now, Marco Polo may have the Mail Safe Express station for sending these items home. However, there are ways to avoid being challenged by new regulations.

To find out what the latest security items are, it's best that you wait until the last week of your vacation and go online to the federal government **www.tsa.gov** Website. These items change with the creativity of those individuals who are attempting to disrupt safe air flights. Once you have eliminated those items from your luggage, you are faced with your total luggage weight and the extra amount for which you will have to pay in penalty charges.

### Solutions to Extra Weight

A number of individuals have routinely sent certain overweight items home to themselves by the local postal system. The author's experience has been poor when he chose to send valuable items home by land and sea by foreign mail. People somehow were able to open the packages and take things of value for themselves.

We are accustomed to the high standards of our own postal system or private systems like UPS or FedEx. I recommend that you use UPS, DSL, or FedEx.

### A Smooth Takeoff

Marco Polo Airport provides two levels of moving to the departing aircraft. The departure terminal on the second floor has a number of gates that use the flexible ramps, allowing passengers to walk directly onto the aircraft.

A number of airlines have passengers move to the ground floor to their gates. Passengers load onto long aircraft buses that take them to the planes where they climb aboard the portable stairways used in many smaller airports in the United States.

## Railroad Station Departures

You will notice huge crowds at Santa Lucia Station if you leave or arrive on Saturday or Sunday afternoon. Remember, Venice can be like going to Disneyland for many Italians and most arrive by train on weekends. They come to spend the day or sometimes two days and a night.

## Luggage for Train Departures

There are porters in front of the station to help you carry your bags onto the train. Remember, there is a strong security concern when a bag or suitcase is left in the middle of the station. If you have several hours to wait, you should take your luggage to the baggage storage. There will be a charge; however, it's worth it.

## Disabled Travelers

Wheelchair travelers are well taken care of on Italian railroads. It is important, however, to give a twenty-four-hour notice to the customer services office. If you are traveling from Venice to Rome, you will be met with a wheelchair lift device that lifts you and your chair up to the level of the car. You will be helped with your luggage. When you arrive at the Rome station, there will be another lift device to lower you and your chair to the platform. Remember, this all requires notifying the appropriate railroad staff twenty-four hours ahead.

# *2008 Venice* Update

All of the sights in Venice Easy Sightseeing remain basically the same. Obviously, the economy of the world is constantly changing prices of food, lodging and visitor services. The research of this book has focused primarily on how to best locate,see the sights and move about the buildings. The following changes relating to the services in Venice were current within a month of printing this edition.

**General changes as of September 2008 are;**

Vaporetto boat ticket price changed to 6,50 euros for a single one-way fare for a one hour duration. Boat #82 will be changed to Boat #2 for its route on the grand canal and around the southern coast of the Venice Islands.

Check hppt/www.actv.it for further changes.

Current prices of Operas, Concerts, and Play venues can be found at http/www.venice opera.it, http/www,operahouse.it., and http/www.teatrofenice.it.

Prices and exhibits of the following museums and galleries can be found at http/www.museicivcivenziani.it. Ca'Pesaro, Doges Palace, Clock Tower, Carlo Goldini's House, Ca'Rezzonico

Museum, Glass Museum and the Museum of Natural History at Ca'Pesaro.

Palazzo Contarini del Bovolo near Realto is temporarilly closed for repairs. Call before visiting.

# *Acknowledgements*

We would like to thank those visitors to Venice who pointed out the problems they encountered. We particularly thought of them when we described alternative easy routes and hints on how to avoid and bypass those problems when we visited this, our favorite city.

We also want to thank those organizations and their staffs who provided invaluable information, pictures, and maps to make the book as attractive and informative as possible.

➢ The Artistic Design Director of Holiday Books, Ms. Iris Aguirre, for her skills and constant striving for beauty and ease of reading.
➢ Lucia Baracco, one of the administrators of the External Relations and Communication Department of the Comune di Veneia, for providing Venice accessibility information to assist those adventurous travelers in wheelchairs who required assistance in finding buildings and moving through them in meaningful ways.
➢ Laura Bonam of Booksurge who completed the final design of the text and images.
➢ Anna Maria Mandracchia of Venice Tourist Board, who provided final editing.

- ➤ Roberta Valmarana, Tourist Board of Venice, who provided access to archives for pictures.
- ➤ Katia De Franceschi, Informahandicap, Comune of Venice, who provided invaluable information on how much of a commitment the people of Venice have made to the comfort and development of the disabled.
- ➤ Cristian Pigozzio, Venetian concierge "supreme" who helped the author to live in and love the nature of Venice.
- ➤ Mr. Jack Joyce, president of ITMB map company of Canada, for permission to use ITMB's map of Venice for artistic appeal and guidance of visitors to Venice.
- ➤ Rick Steve and Laura Van Deventer for permission to use their map of the Grand Canal of Venice.
- ➤ The staff of BookSurge.com (subsidiary of Amazon.com) for their expertise and guidance through the publication of *Venice, Easy Sightseeing*.
- ➤ Travis Craine, publishing consultant; Aaron Voelker, account manager; Ms. Sarah Southerland, editorial products manager; and our skillful editor, Ms. Gail Chadwick.

# *About the author*

Donald Bowling earned his Bachelor and Master Degrees at UCLA in California. He majored in human development and minored in, world history and art. He also fulfilled California's requirements for public school teaching and administrative credentials. He taught and was school principal in public schools and California State Hospitals.

His career continued to focus on developmentally disabled adults and children with the Department of Developmental Services. His career's expertese allowed him to participate in the development of building accessibility standards for the disabled. He retired as Chief of the Clinical Services Division of California State Hospitals and Developmental Centers.

Bowling's interest in world history and art led to years of visiting Venice, Florence and Rome. He began writing to meet the needs of middle aged, senior and disabled tourists in Italy when he discovered the physical challenges of touring the aged buildings of these cities.

# *Index*

# *Image Credits*

**Holiday Travel Books** wishes to thank the following publishers, organizations and photographers for their assistance in the preparation of this book.

**Holiday Travel Books** photographer Ethel Von Wileth for the photographs on the front and back cover. Her other photographs of Venice are shown on the following pages_5, 6, 41, 45, 69, 70, 71, 86, 113, 114, 132, 143, 155, 170, 203 and 211.

Venice Accessibility, arch Lucia Baracco, Comune di Venezia, Direzione Gabinetto del Sindaco e Relazioni e Comunicazione, Informahandicap Services; Marciano area, Rialto Area, Frari Area, Dorsoduro Area and S. Stefano Area. Pages 215, 219, 223, 227 and 231.

Archive pictures from Azienda di Promozione Turistica della Provincia di Venezia, Roberta Valmarana. Archive pictures on pages_12, 14, 19, 34, 44, 45, 85, 100, 162, 182, 196, 200 and 204.

Sections of ITMB Venice Map, C. (copyright) ITMB Publishing Ltd., permission by ITMB president, Mr. Jack Joyce, 530 W. Broadway, Vancouver, BC, Canada, V5ZIEQ9, shown on pages _vii, 15, 48, 74, 89, 103, 117, 135, 146, 158, 172, 181, 191, 198, 207 and 245.

Map of the Grand Canal and parts of Venice C. 2006 *Europe through the Back Door* from Rick Steve. Reprinted by permission of Rick Steve and Avalon Travel Publishing. Shown on pages_ viii, ix.

Alessandro Zanchini, Davide Toffanin and Renato Greco of Servizio Videocomunicazione, Citta di Venezia. La Fenice Opera House page_133 and Calatrava Bridge on page 189.